Harvard
Business
Review

ON

MOTIVATING PEOPLE

THE HARVARD BUSINESS REVIEW PAPERBACK SERIES

The series is designed to bring today's managers and professionals the fundamental information they need to stay competitive in a fast-moving world. From the preeminent thinkers whose work has defined an entire field to the rising stars who will redefine the way we think about business, here are the leading minds and landmark ideas that have established the *Harvard Business Review* as required reading for ambitious businesspeople in organizations around the globe.

Other books in the series:

Harvard Business Review

ON

MOTIVATING PEOPLE

Copyright 2003
Harvard Business School Publishing Corporation
All rights reserved
Printed in the United States of America
10 09 08 07   10 9 8 7 6

The *Harvard Business Review* articles in this collection are available as
individual reprints. Discounts apply to quantity purchases. For information and ordering, please contact Customer Service, Harvard Business
School Publishing, Boston, MA 02163. Telephone: (617) 783-7500 or
(800) 988-0886, 8 A.M. to 6 P.M. Eastern Time, Monday through Friday.
Fax: (617) 783-7555, 24 hours a day. E-mail: custserv@hbsp.harvard.edu

978-1-59139-132-6 (ISBN 13)
Library of Congress Cataloging-in-Publication Data
Harvard business review on motivating people.
    p.   cm. — (Harvard business review paperback series)
Includes index.
   ISBN 1-59139-132-6
   1. Employee motivation.   I. Harvard Business School Press.   II.
Harvard business review.   III. Harvard business review paperback
series.
HF5549.5.M63H37   2003
658.3´14—dc21   2003005860
                                                              CIP

Contents

Harvard Business Review

ON

MOTIVATING PEOPLE

Beyond Empowerment

Building a Company of Citizens

BROOK MANVILLE AND JOSIAH OBER

Executive Summary

WE LIVE IN A KNOWLEDGE ECONOMY. The core assets of the modern business enterprise aren't its buildings, machinery, and real estate, but the intelligence, understanding, skills, and experience of its employees. Harnessing the capabilities and commitment of knowledge workers is arguably the central managerial challenge of our time. Unfortunately, it is a challenge that has not yet been met. Corporate ownership structures, governance systems, and incentive programs—despite the enlightened rhetoric of business leaders—remain firmly planted in the industrial age.

In this article, the authors draw on history to lay out a model for a democratic business organization suited to the knowledge economy. Some 2,500 years ago, the city-state of ancient Athens rose to unprecedented political and economic power by giving its citizens a direct

1

voice and an active role in civic governance. The city's uniquely participative system of democracy helped unleash the creativity of the Athenian people and channel it to produce the greatest good for society. The system succeeded in bringing individual initiative and common cause into harmony. And that is precisely the synthesis today's companies need to achieve if they're to realize the full power of their people and thrive in the knowledge economy.

The Athenian model of organizational democracy is just that—a model. It does not provide a simple set of prescriptions for modern managers. What it offers is a window into how sizable groups of people can, in an atmosphere of dignity and trust, successfully govern themselves without resorting to a stifling bureaucracy.

W E LIVE TODAY IN A KNOWLEDGE ECONOMY. The core assets of the modern business enterprise lie not in buildings, machinery, and real estate, but in the intelligence, understanding, skills, and experience of employees. Harnessing the capabilities and commitment of knowledge workers is, it might be argued, the central managerial challenge of our time. Unfortunately, it is a challenge that has not yet been met. Corporate ownership structures, governance systems, and incentive programs—despite the enlightened rhetoric of business leaders—are still firmly planted in the industrial age. We grant ownership rights only to the providers of financial capital, not to the providers of intellectual capital. We govern through small management teams at the top of hierarchies. We motivate people through Pavlovian carrot-and-stick incentives.

It's true that business organizations have become less bureaucratic in recent years and that authority has been pushed down through the ranks. People at lower levels— unit managers, factory workers, customer service representatives—have greater autonomy today than they did a generation ago. But such "empowerment," as it's commonly called, is limited. Workers are able to make decisions about their immediate jobs or to participate in somewhat broader decisions about their own units, but they still have little or no voice in decisions about the direction of the overall company. They remain essentially disenfranchised. It should be no surprise, therefore, that many knowledge workers feel estranged from their organizations—their outlook distrustful, their attitude cynical, their loyalty tenuous.

At the heart of the problem is a lack of adequate models. Although we know how command-and-control management works in an industrial company, we have no working template for a truly democratic system of management—one suited to the knowledge worker's need for and expectation of self-determination and self-government. But if a usable model for a democratic organization does not yet exist in the business world, history offers a compelling, if unexpected, prototype. Some 2,500 years ago, the city-state of ancient Athens rose to unprecedented political and economic power by giving its citizens a direct voice and an active role in civic governance. Although not without its flaws, the city's uniquely participative system of democracy helped unleash the creativity of the Athenian people and channel it in ways that produced the greatest good for the society as a whole. The system succeeded in bringing individual initiative and common cause into harmony. And that is precisely the synthesis that

today's companies need to achieve if they're to realize
the full power of their people and thrive in the knowledge economy.

An Ancient Model

It is the year 480 BC. Dawn is breaking over the small
Greek island of Salamis, just off the coast of Athens.
Thousands of Athenian citizens huddle on slender,
wooden galleys, clutching weapons and oars. Facing
them are hundreds of powerful, hulking warships, the
majestic fighting navy of the Persian Empire. That force
is poised to complete the Persian takeover of the Greek
mainland and its prize jewel, the flourishing city of
Athens. Across the narrow strait, on a commanding hill,
sits the Great King of Persia himself, eager to witness the
culmination of years of preparation. He expects that victory will come easily. After all, the Athenians are a ragtag
bunch. They do not even have a king of their own to dis-
pense orders.

Yet by the time dusk falls, the Persian king's grandiose
plans are in ruins. The Athenians have successfully carried out a bold and innovative battle plan, using the
agility of their lighter ships, together with their deep
knowledge of local geography and weather, to outmaneu-
ver and ultimately defeat their far more powerful foe.
Spurred by a deep sense of civic duty, the Athenians have
fought together with especial valor, and their superior
ingenuity, motivation, and commitment carry the day.
Against all odds, a small community of 30,000 citizens
defeats a colossal, monarchic military machine.

In the years following their great victory at Salamis,
the Athenians were quick to exploit their advantage,
steadily expanding their influence across the Aegean Sea.

Skillfully combining diplomacy and military might, and resiliently rebounding from setbacks, they built the first great Greek empire. They not only kept the Persians at bay, but swept pirates from the sea, making the Aegean a safer place to trade. Commerce boomed, and many individuals prospered. Private and public wealth soared, as the city-state collected the modern-day equivalent of billions of dollars in taxes and tributes from a rapidly expanding group of subject states.

At the same time, Athens spawned a cultural florescence the likes of which the world had never seen. The atmosphere of the democratic city was open, experimental, and entrepreneurial. Philosophers, artists, scientists, and poets from across the Mediterranean world flocked to Athens's academies, workshops, and public squares. Not only was the great Parthenon built, but many other masterpieces of architecture and sculpture were created too. Moral philosophy came into being, the craft of history writing emerged, and drama became a great art form. Scientists developed new theories about everything from the atomic structure of matter to the relationship of the earth to heavenly bodies.

Underpinning all the achievements was a system of governance based on personal freedom, collective action, and an open, democratic culture. Athens was at heart a community of citizens—a "politeia," to use the Greek word—and each of those citizens had both the right and the obligation to play an active role in the society's governance. (Although the Athenian conception of democracy marked a historic leap forward in civic and political thinking, it is important to note that it did not extend to the enfranchisement of women or immigrants, much less the freeing of chattel slaves.) Our emaciated modern conception of democracy makes it difficult to understand the richness of the original Athenian concept. What we call "citizenship" today—an essentially passive legal status involving only minimal civic obligations and relying on a distant and entrenched governing elite—is but a shadow of the Athenian politeia.

The Architecture of Citizenship

What made the democracy of ancient Athens so successful, and why does it stand as a good model for businesses today? First, the system was not imposed on the Athenian people, but rather it grew organically from their own needs, beliefs, and actions—it was as much a spirit of governance as a set of rules or laws. Any managerial structure that is to have true meaning to knowledge workers must also emerge naturally from their own aspirations and initiatives. And second, the system was holistic—it was successful because it informed all aspects of the society, just as a productive corporate culture must inform all aspects of an organization and its management. The Athenian democracy encompassed *participatory structures* for making decisions, resolving disputes, and managing activities; a set of *communal values* that defined people's relationships with one another; and an array of *practices of engagement* that ensured the broad participation of the entire citizenry. By looking more carefully at this architecture of citizenship, we gain hints of what the business organization of the future might look like.

PARTICIPATORY STRUCTURES

The Athenian system of governance had what might be called a radically flat organization—much flatter than even the leanest of corporate structures today. A set of clearly defined and universally understood processes and institutions—including councils, courts, assemblies, and executive offices—served to minimize hierarchy, inhibit the development of a ruling class, and engage citizens in governance and jurisprudence. In addition to taking part in local policy making, every adult male Athenian had the opportunity to attend the great citizen assembly, which met almost weekly to debate and vote on matters of importance, from financing the construction of a new road to fighting a war. The assembly was steered by a council of 500 citizens whose membership rotated annually. The councilors took turns setting the assembly's agenda and presiding over its deliberations.

To ensure that the decisions of the populace would be executed swiftly and well, the Athenian governance structure also included teams of "executives"—generals, administrators, managers—who were selected by election or lottery. Turnover in executive positions was systematic: At some point in their lives, most of Athens's 30,000 citizens had the opportunity to participate as a leader. Individual performance was carefully monitored, and outgoing executives were rewarded or punished accordingly—

People with expertise came forward whenever their skills were needed, without becoming part of any standing bureaucracy.

but only by their peers, the body of citizens themselves. The administration of justice was similarly open and participatory. Citizen arbitrators settled most conflicts, but when arbitration failed or the crime was particularly serious, juries representing the entire citizenry made the judgments and set the penalties.

Transparent procedural rules governed judicial and policy-making processes, keeping them simple, fair, and flexible. But the processes also allowed, even encouraged, passion and emotion. Many decisions made by the citizens were literally matters of life and death; no one was ejected from meetings for speaking loudly or heatedly— as long as the rights of others were respected. Expertise in technical matters was deeply valued, but the concept of professionalism played little part in the system. Amateur engagement was seen as preferable to professional management because it encouraged the constant sharing of fresh viewpoints and knowledge. It was expected that people with expertise in a particular area would come forward whenever their skills were needed, without becoming part of any standing bureaucracy. Laws and policies were stated in plain language; professional prosecutors and lawyers were unknown. Time limits on debate in courts and assemblies allowed each citizen to have his voice heard and prevented any bloc from dominating the proceedings. And voting on policy was open and mostly "by consensus," though secret ballots were employed for judicial decisions to ensure fairness.

In combination, these democratic structures ensured that no obstacles or barriers would arise to separate the Athenians from their government. More important, they reflected the people's deep trust in their own ability to chart the course of their state. Think how different such a notion is from the beliefs that underlie corporate management structures today. In most companies, major decisions continue to be made by small, insular elites behind the closed doors of executive offices and conference rooms. Tightly scripted planning, budgeting, and approval processes deter rather than encourage free thinking and honest debate. The entire shape of the modern company reflects a fundamental distrust of its members—a distrust that, as recent American business scandals have shown, can all too easily give rise to a malignant arrogance.

COMMUNAL VALUES

Establishing democratic structures is not enough, of course. People do not walk miles to attend meetings, forsake precious time to play temporary executive roles, or risk their lives in wars merely for the sake of "structures." For ancient Athenians, as for knowledge workers today, motivation came from a higher purpose—from a sense of shared ownership in their community's destiny. A distinctive set of values made the personal communal and the communal personal. In most companies today, by contrast, there is a tension between the employee's individual will and the will of the organization. Management is forever arbitrating the bounds between personal freedom and the corporate interest. In Athens, there was no such tension. The interest of the citizen was indistinguishable from the interest of the government.

How many knowledge workers today would automatically embrace the company's interest as their own?

The society placed the highest possible value on individuality, diligently protecting each person's right to self-determination, equality of opportunity, and security. Every citizen was free to—and encouraged to—express himself publicly, debate and dissent, and participate actively in all decisions that would materially affect him. But he was also free to pursue his private interests; he was not expected to engage constantly in public matters, but to contribute only when his skills and perspectives were needed. All citizens were given an equal chance to fulfill their personal potential while making their greatest possible contributions to the society. Finally, each citizen was secure, protected from the physical coercion and verbal abuse that would have made it impossible to enjoy either freedom or equality. As members of a community devoted to the common good, citizens were expected to band together not only to guarantee their collective security from external threats, but to guarantee the security of each individual from vicious behavior on the part of any aberrant internal member or group. The public welfare depended on the protection of each of the community's members.

A second set of Athenian values, balancing those that focused on individuality, centered on community, on the belief that the people *are* the state. So deeply held was this concept that it was embedded in the language: "Athens" was only the name of a place; the name of the community was "the Athenians." The physical manifestations of the city paled in importance to its people. The historian Thucydides memorably quotes an Athenian general's address to the citizenry on the eve of a great battle: "Not ships, not walls, but men make our city." How many knowledge workers today, hearing a similar pronouncement from their company's top management, would believe it? How many would automatically embrace the company's interest as their own?

Critical to the day-to-day integration of individual and community was a third set of values having to do with moral reciprocity. The sense of moral reciprocity provided the all-important link between "What's in it for me?" and "What's in it for us?" Its essence was the shared belief that engagement in the life of the community was educational in the broadest sense: It gave each individual the chance to become better, to grow wiser, and to fully develop his talents. As a citizen, you owed the community your best effort; the community, in return, owed you every opportunity to fulfill your potential. By providing unfettered opportunity to each of its members, the society understood that it would arrive at the best solutions to problems facing everyone.

On the surface, moral reciprocity may seem like an ancient version of what in business has come to be called "the employability contract": An employer promises to further the employee's professional development (and thus career prospects) in return for the employee's commitment to perform at the highest possible level throughout his or her tenure. There are, however, two significant differences between the modern concept of employability and the Athenian concept of moral reciprocity. First, employability does not foster long-term loyalty—indeed, it envisions each worker's likely departure. Employability is a short-term bargain that assumes a conflict between the interest of the community and that of its individual members. Athenian citizens, by contrast, could not ordinarily be "fired" from their organization, nor were they likely to leave it for any but the direst of reasons. Whether modern global business can (or should) ever return to a goal of long-term employment remains to be seen. But the contract between the individual and community will be richer and more productive for both if it has a meaningful chance of durability.

The second difference between employability contracts and moral reciprocity is less obvious but perhaps more important. Whereas moral reciprocity is integrally tied to a broader dependency between the individual and the community, employability is simply a quid pro quo understanding about working and learning on the job. Without the chance to meaningfully participate in steering one's own destiny, without the opportunity to gain the sincere respect of one's peers, without an honest stake in making the community more successful through one's own work and ideas, employability can quickly decay into generic training programs or bogus choices among short lists of uninspiring assignments. Narrowly construed employability contracts will motivate knowledge workers only so far.

PRACTICES OF ENGAGEMENT

The structure and values of Athenian democracy outlined above provided the framework for citizenship. Ultimately, however, citizenship must be expressed in action—in day-to-day practices—or it will quickly degenerate into bureaucracy, routines, and self-interest. An organization's practices define its culture, how work gets done. To the Athenians, though, the practices of democracy were not just about "doing citizenship" but also about "learning citizenship." They continually refined their understanding of the workings of democracy through their actions and interactions in public squares, in leadership roles, and in jury trials.

The practices that animated the Athenian system can be broken out into subgroups, though it is essential to think about them in their totality—and as embedded in the structures and values to which they gave life.

Practices of access ensured that every citizen had free and equal opportunity to participate in self-governance. Athenians volunteered in both making and executing decisions, sharing their knowledge by participating in forums and initiatives at both the local and statewide level. The rotation of roles was crucial to the dynamism of governance, enabling all citizens to have opportunities to lead, to assume executive positions, and in general to take turns at ruling and being ruled.

Practices of process were essential in ensuring that deliberations, decision making, and execution were carried out in ways that were consistent, fair, and timely. Citizens sought consensus, making decisions and judgments based on trust among well-intentioned individuals (the polar opposite of today's partisan politics). All governmental and judicial processes were transparent, ensuring that every decision was based on information freely offered and supported by clearly expressed reasons. The populace also believed in making decisions swiftly; citizens maintained a sense of urgency in bringing debates to a conclusion. Finally, it was expected that all would support and, as necessary, assist in executing decisions, regardless of one's point of view prior to the final vote.

Practices of consequence ensured that citizens did not come to see process as an end in itself (a sure recipe for bureaucracy), but rather maintained a focus on achieving practical and concrete results. Fundamental to the society's emphasis on outcomes was the concept of merit; the people strove to ensure that every decision was based on the best argument, never on the position, privilege, or prejudice of those deciding. Another cherished concept was accountability—accepting personal responsibility for respecting the values of the citizen culture in all decision-making and executive settings, supporting those values in one's own conduct, and accepting peers' judgments about one's performance. Finally, the Athenians considered it an obligation to challenge the process—to seek to reverse misguided policies, appeal bad decisions, and call attention to, and act upon, misbehavior that threatened the community or any of its members.

Each of these three sets of practices was governed by an overarching group of *jurisdiction practices,* which ensured that every decision was made in the right place, by the right people, and at the right time. The community believed that decisions should be made by those with the greatest knowledge of the issues and the greatest stake in the consequences. This meant that technical decisions tended to be left to experts; decisions about battle strategy, for example, were reserved for generals. Decisions of great consequence, from levying taxes to declaring war, demanded full-scale debate by the society as a whole. Other, more mundane decisions—scheduling festivals or resolving disputes between neighbors, for example—were made locally. So precious was the possession of citizenship for Athenians that the entire citizen body had the jurisdiction to consider any proposal to confer citizenship upon a foreigner.

The culture of citizenship created by the Athenians— with its interplay of structures, values, and practices— encouraged every person to zealously pursue individual excellence and at the same time created, through shared processes of self-governance, an emotional commitment to efforts for the common good. This kind of "both/and" thinking has recently been promoted by Jim Collins and other management thinkers. It seeks to break the conflict between self-interest and corporate interest. Pericles, the Athenian statesman, expressed the essence of this attitude. Every citizen, he said, was "the rightful lord and owner of his own person," exhibiting "an exceptional grace and versatility." And, he went on, thanks to their politeia and their entire way of life, the citizens were collectively able to be a great and powerful community.

Indeed, this "school to the rest of Greece," as Pericles called his city, was the envy of and an object of fear to its enemies. One of Athens's rivals spoke in awe of how the motivation of its citizens yielded outstanding performance: "They regard their bodies as expendable for their city's sake, and each man cultivates his own intelligence, for doing something notable for the common cause . . . Of the Athenians alone it may be said, they begin to possess something almost as soon as they desire it, so quickly are they able to act upon something once they have made a decision . . . and when they are successful, they regard that success as nothing compared to what they will do next."

Looking Ahead

The Athenian model of organizational democracy is just that—a model. It does not provide a simple set of prescriptions for modern managers. It does, however, offer a window into how sizable groups of people can successfully govern themselves with dignity and trust and without resorting to a stifling bureaucracy. Most important, it shows the need to combine structures, values, and practices in a coherent, self-sustaining system. Simply creating forums or processes for group decision making will not be enough—half-hearted measures will only amplify employee cynicism. Building and sustaining a company of citizens requires a genuine change in organizational and managerial culture.

Most of today's workers are familiar with the basic values and structures of democracy, and most have experience with some forms of communal action at work, whether it's serving on self-managed teams, reaching decisions through consensus building, or sharing leadership responsibilities. The idea of moving toward a more democratic structure should not, therefore, be a foreign

one. Still, what we're talking about is a radical change in
the corporate mind-set, and complications abound. Consider a few of the most obvious: Technological advances,
demographic shifts, and the increasing globalization of
markets have dispersed workforces, undermined traditional assumptions about job security and employee loyalty, and created far more open markets for labor. The
very definition of an "employee" has grown fuzzy, as
companies rely increasingly on freelancers, contractors,
and temporary workers.

One of the first hurdles a company will need to clear is
simply to define what constitutes a "citizen." What are
the benefits, rights, and responsibilities that go along
with formal citizenship in an organization? Should limited citizenship be available, with lesser rights and
responsibilities? Should contractors and partners be
given some form of citizenship? How should different
levels of citizenship be managed? How should ownership
rights and other rewards be distributed? These are hard
questions, and every company will need to answer them
in its own way, taking account of its size, circumstances,
and goals.

One thing, however, is certain: The practice of citizenship cannot be imposed from above. It must grow out of
the actions and beliefs of the citizens themselves. The
transition to a more democratic business organization
will thus take time, requiring many experiments and
many successes and failures. While an organization's
managers will necessarily play key roles in establishing
basic goals and values—as a series of great leaders did
for Athens—they must also have the courage to take
their turn in being led, as the self-confidence of the citizenry grows. It is a process that must never cease: The
experience of democracy must continually refine the
practice of democracy.

Pericles told his fellow Athenians that "future ages will wonder at us, even as the present age wonders at us now." Over two thousand years later, his bold prediction rings true. But our attention to Athens should not be limited to wonder. It should encompass emulation as well.

Originally published in January 2003
Reprint R0301C

How to Motivate Your Problem People

NIGEL NICHOLSON

Executive Summary

MANAGERS WHO MOTIVATE WITH INCENTIVES and
the power of their vision and passion succeed only in
energizing employees who want to be motivated. So
how do you motivate intractable employees—the ones
who never do what you want and also take up all your
time? According to Nigel Nicholson, you can't: Individuals must motivate themselves. Nicholson advocates a
method that turns conventional approaches to motivation
upside down.

Instead of pushing solutions on problem employees,
the manager should pull solutions out of them by creating
circumstances in which the employees can channel
their motivation toward achievable goals. That means
addressing any obstacles—possibly even the manager's
own demotivating style—that might be hindering the
employees. The author's method demands that a

19

manager take charge of a difficult situation and resolve it. An investment of time is required, but it will bring the manager to a resolution sooner than other means would. Using detailed examples, Nicholson walks the reader through his method, pointing out potential pitfalls along the way.

First, the manger creates a rich picture of the problem person. Second, the manager exercises flexibility and reframes goals so that the employee can meet them. Third, in a carefully staged, face-to-face conversation, the manager meets with the problem employee on neutral ground.

Whether a problem is solved or simply resolved, the payoffs from using this method extend beyond the specific employees who have been difficult to motivate. Besides increasing a manager's chances of motivating problem people, the method can inspire an entire team by signaling that the organization deals with difficult people rather than discarding them.

Everyone knows that good managers motivate with the power of their vision, the passion of their delivery, and the compelling logic of their reasoning. Add in the proper incentives, and people will enthusiastically march off in the right direction.

It's a great image, promoted in stacks of idealistic leadership books. But something is seriously wrong with it: Such a strategy works with only a fraction of employees and a smaller fraction of managers. Why? For one thing, few executives are particularly gifted at rallying the troops. Exhorting most managers to become Nelson Mandelas or Winston Churchills imbues them with little more than a sense of guilt and inadequacy. For another, all available evidence suggests that external incentives—be they pep talks, wads of cash, or even the threat of unpleasant consequences—have limited impact. The people who might respond to such inducements are already up and running. It's the other folks who are the problem. And, as all managers know from painful experience, when it comes to managing people, the 80-20 rule applies: The most intractable employees take up a disproportionate amount of one's time and energy.

So how do you get these people to follow your lead? How do you get them energized and committed in such a way that they not only support your initiatives but carry them out?

After 30 years of studying business organizations and advising executives, I have concluded that these are precisely the wrong questions to ask. That's because, as it turns out, you can't motivate these problem people: Only they themselves can. Your job is to create the circumstances in which their inherent motivation—the natural commitment and drive that most people have—is freed and channeled toward achievable goals. That approach requires an entirely different managerial mind-set. Achieving this shift in perspective is anything but easy. But it's your best hope for getting the most out of your difficult employees. And if you succeed, your task won't be prodding or coaxing these people; it will be removing barriers—including, quite possibly, your own demotivating management style.

A Familiar Problem

Let's look at a couple of situations that will surely resonate with most managers. First, consider the problem facing Annette. (Though the cases in this article are real, the names and identifying details have been changed.) She is a senior designer at a large publishing and graphic design business, with dotted-line responsibility for Colin, a project team member. Always something of a maverick, Colin nonetheless has a good work history. But the team is feeling the heat because the company restructured it to reduce costs and speed turnaround times. And Colin's behavior is becoming increasingly problematic, or so Annette and Dave, the project manager and Colin's other boss, see it. Colin seems to be shirking work, and when he does complete assignments, he doesn't report back to his bosses. To Annette, Colin's behavior doesn't just reflect his inherent disregard for rules and procedures; it also signifies a reluctance to take on further assignments. After discussing the situation with Dave, Annette decides that she will be the one to talk to Colin because she has the better relationship with him.

Annette's strategy is to motivate Colin by appealing to his sense of responsibility to the project team. When she meets with him and tries to get him to accept this line of reasoning, Colin agrees to do what Annette wants. But she doesn't get the feeling that her argument has made any impact. In her opinion, Colin is in his comfort zone: He supports the other team members, even helps them to solve their problems, but he does so at the expense of fulfilling his own responsibilities. Annette wonders whether Colin has become a misfit in the new structure and will have to leave. Perhaps she should give him a formal warning at his annual appraisal. Or maybe she should transfer him to a less demanding job, in effect demoting him.

Here's another case. Paolo works in Eastern Europe as a country manager for an international property developer. George, a chartered accountant with an MBA, is a direct report whose job is to sell plots of land and develop strategic alliances with local companies. George is fairly new to this position, having previously worked in a back-office role overseeing customer accounts. Although George is pleasant and enthusiastic, his performance is subpar and shows no signs of improvement. In fact, George has yet to sell a single parcel of land. In his dealings with potential partners, the garrulous George acts as though his bonhomie is all he needs to cut a deal. And the deals he does manage to make turn out to be ill considered and costly.

Because of these issues, Paolo meets with George several times to try to get him to change his ways. George responds with encouraging smiles, plausible excuses, and a commitment to Paolo that things will change, but nothing does. In the final analysis, Paolo decides, George is slippery and lazy. Despite his promises, George refuses to adopt a different negotiating style, and he obviously isn't prepared to do the detailed research necessary to appraise a deal. Exasperated, Paolo decides to issue George an ultimatum: Improve your game or get out. But firing George would be an expensive option; people with his background and skills are difficult to find in this part of the world.

Poor Paolo. He can almost smell the failure likely to result from a confrontation. He'll continue to get reassurances from George, but will he ever get George to change his ways and be accountable for his performance? Poor Annette. If only she could convince Colin to improve his attitude, she could hold on to a potentially valuable team member. But no matter how reasonable Annette's argument is, will she be able to get Colin to behave differently?

The Mistakes Managers Make

These two cases share some qualities that often bedevil
executives in their attempts to motivate problem people.
For instance, Annette and Paolo believe that they just
need the right sales pitch to turn around Colin and
George. Each boss thinks, "If I can only get this person to
listen, he'll see the logic of my position." This approach,
something I call "tell and sell," is based on a profound
fallacy many of us buy into: Other people have the same
thought processes we do, and, consequently, they *have* to
accept the good sense of what we're saying.

But each of us has a unique profile of motivational
drivers, values, and biases, and we have different ideas
about what is reasonable. This frequent mismatch of perceptions leads to another common problem with managerial attempts at motivation: the futile and prolonged
game of tag, with a manager repeatedly trying to slap
some motivation onto the problem employee. The
employee either evades the boss's attempts or, if tagged,
quickly wriggles free. Think of Colin avoiding his bosses.
Think of George and his elusive promises. Every manager
is familiar with the "Sure, boss" meetings that end with
an apparent resolution but ultimately result in more
of the same old problem and the person not changing
one jot.

In fact, such unsatisfactory outcomes shouldn't surprise managers like Annette and Paolo. In trying to con-
vert Colin and George into different kinds of people,
they—like most managers dealing with problem employees—have set themselves an impossible goal. A fundamental rule of management is that you can't change people's character; you can't even control their actions most
of the time. Change comes from within or not at all.

A New Approach to Motivation

So if Annette and Paolo have approached their problems
in the wrong way, what is the right way? I propose a relatively simple method I have seen work time and again. It
involves shifting the responsibility for motivation from
subject to object, from boss to subordinate. Crucially, it
also involves a shift in perspective: The manager needs to
look at the employee not as a problem to be solved but as
a person to be understood. (For a discussion of this
change in perspective, see "Decentering: The Art at the
Heart of Motivation" at the end of this article.) My
method is based on a handful of principles:

EVERYONE HAS MOTIVATIONAL ENERGY

Although many problem employees display a marked
lack of drive and commitment in their jobs, these qualities are usually alive and well in other areas of their lives.
Certainly, not all people
are going to feel the same
passion for their work
that they do for their hob-
bies or other outside
interests. But it's a mis-
take to write off a problem employee as simply unmotivated. Most workers have the potential to engage with
their work in a way that furthers managerial goals.

*Instead of pushing solutions
on people with the
force of your argument, pull
solutions out of them.*

THIS ENERGY IS OFTEN BLOCKED IN THE
WORKPLACE

A variety of factors can block people's natural motivation. For example, impediments may appear suddenly

because of new stresses at home or may accumulate incrementally over years, the product of frustrated dreams or broken promises at work. The effect is to transform a person's positive energy into negative attitudes and behavior—or simply to divert it into nonwork activities. One of the most common blockages occurs when employees feel that their bosses don't really care about them. For this or other reasons, problem employees usually don't much like their managers. And chances are that the sentiments are mutual—which makes conventional pep talks about improving performance come across as insincere, at best.

REMOVING BLOCKAGES REQUIRES EMPLOYEE PARTICIPATION

To motivate an employee to work toward your goals, you need to take a judolike approach: Find the person's locus of energy and leverage it to achieve your ends. Instead of pushing solutions on people with the force of your argument, pull solutions out of them. Turning the tables gets employees' attention at the very least; ideally, it prompts them to clear the obstacles impeding their motivation. To accomplish this, you may have to rethink what your problem employees can reasonably be motivated to do. But the approach will help you get the best from them, whatever their abilities and skills.

Let's look at potential objections to the method I'm proposing. "This all sounds too soft and squishy to me," you might say. Or, "I've got a business to run and have neither the inclination nor the time to serve as the sympathetic shrink to a bunch of 'blocked' employees who refuse to get with the program."

First, while this method is based on empathy, it is anything but soft. It demands that a manager take charge of a difficult situation and resolve it. In fact, the truly spongy method is what you are probably using now: either ignoring your problem employees or repeatedly and unsuccessfully trying to convince them that they should improve their performance. Although in exasperation you may end up sacking them, that's a sign of failure, not firmness. Second, my method does require an investment of time, but it is an investment that should get you to a resolution of the problem sooner than other means would. That's because it requires you to move beyond the point of "stuckness" that characterizes so many relationships with problem people.

Keep in mind that this approach is designed to create a resolution—not necessarily a solution—to the problem you face. While the method should help you avoid some common pitfalls in trying to motivate difficult employees (see "Seven Hazards in Handling Problem People" at the end of this article), you won't be able to transform every unmotivated employee. And even if an employee's behavior does change, you may not get exactly what you originally wanted. But the three-step method I propose will put an end to the evasions, repetitions, and broken promises. And it will likely yield options that you hadn't even considered. At the very least, it will drive you to a moment of truth, a point at which you and the employee together can see a path to the goal you have set—or agree that no solution is possible.

Step 1: Create a Rich Picture

Tom has been struggling to help Jack improve his performance. But with each warning, Jack, who is naturally shy, just seems to get quieter. In the end, without fuss or ceremony, Tom tells Jack that things aren't working out and he'll have to leave the company. In the days that follow,

Jack's former colleagues are abuzz with talk about his sudden dismissal—and what they've just learned about his situation. It turns out that both of Jack's parents had recently died after lingering and debilitating illnesses. Until now, no one, including Tom, knew what he had been going through.

Jack's case is extreme, but it illustrates a phenomenon distressingly common in business. A problem employee is taken through the usual appraisal routines and management discussions and then is dismissed—sometimes after years of unproductive performance. Shortly thereafter, the line manager learns from the person's former peers about something that may have been behind the poor performance. The manager never knew about it because of the employee's pride or natural reserve—or because the individual disliked or mistrusted the manager.

The first step thus requires that a manager work to understand where a problem employee is coming from: What drives that person? What blocks those drives? What might happen if the impediments are removed? But that isn't all. Two other factors also figure in the equation: you, as the boss, and the context within which the problem is occurring.

Let's start with the employee. How can Tom know so little about what is affecting Jack's work? How well does Annette understand Colin? What does Paolo really know about George? Clearly, these managers need more information. It can come from peers, subordinates, or previous bosses. Much of the data will come, however, from problem employees themselves. You need to have a series of informal conversations—at the water cooler, over lunch, at social events—that will give you insight into what your employees are really about. What does the world look like from where the employee sits? How have his expectations and desires been molded by key past experiences? What passions govern his choices? What stifles these passions in the workplace? This may sound difficult, but in executive classes I teach, I find that people can learn these things about one another in a ten-minute interview, if they ask the right questions. After all, we often have these conversations at dinner parties; we just rarely have them at work. What you discover will likely surprise you. A test of this would be asking problem employees to describe themselves. It's almost a certainty that they would use different words from the ones you might use.

You may be the cause of your employee's lack of motivation; for some reason, you are bringing out the worst rather than the best in the person you're trying to help.

These informal conversations are the starting point in effectively motivating problem people. For example, Annette learns through some asking around that Colin, outside work, is building a house. No motivation problem there!

Next, you need to look at your own role in the problem you've been trying to solve, especially because direct bosses are the most potent source of employee dissatisfaction and the chief reason people quit their jobs. In fact, you may be the main, if inadvertent, cause of your employee's lack of motivation; for one reason or another, you are bringing out the worst rather than the best in the person you're trying to help. You will have to do some honest soul-searching. And you'll need to do the same sort of asking around that helped you fill out your picture of the employee. Your problem employee may be uncomfortable talking about his or her perception of you, but over time you may even be able to piece together a picture—probably unflattering—of how you are viewed. Even if that picture seems unfair and inaccurate, remember: If something is perceived as real, it is real in its consequences.

Others can provide additional information. Paolo, in discussing George with another manager, complains: "He acts like I'm persecuting him, if you can believe that." Imagine Paolo's surprise when the colleague, who is a friend, responds, "Well, Paolo, I'm sure he's wrong about persecution, but you do come across as a bit of a bully sometimes."

What you learn may convince you that your relationship with the problem employee is dysfunctional beyond repair, at which point you should abandon the method and hand over the motivation task to someone else. More likely, though, the way you interact with a problem employee—for example, something as basic as the way you talk to that person—is simply a turn-off. What works fine with your other reports is hopelessly wrong for this individual. Needless to say, that can be a chastening realization, and many managers find it hard to face.

Finally, you need to analyze the context. Is something about the current situation bringing out the worst in the employee—and maybe in you? Annette thinks Colin's performance has deteriorated because of the increased demands the restructuring has placed on the project team. But Annette's under pressure, too. Are Colin's actions bothering Annette more than they would otherwise because of the stress she faces? Do her reactions to him, paradoxically, add to Colin's stress, creating a vicious cycle?

Once you embark on this kind of fact-finding mission, you'll see that you didn't have sufficient data to solve your problem. Quite possibly, your dislike has gotten in the way of getting to know the problem employee. Furthermore, you probably didn't think your own behavior could be partly to blame. And you probably haven't gone out of your way to look for situational factors that might in some sense excuse the employee's shortcomings. It's much easier simply to label people as difficult than to figure out how they got that way or implicate yourself in the mess.

But if you can break out of this narrow mind-set, you're more likely to get the employee to perform better. And you'll probably rethink what you wanted to achieve with this problem employee in the first place.

Step 2: Reframe Your Goals

Hans runs a division of a Swiss brokerage business. Luca is a member of a 12-person back-office team there that, although it processes customer accounts, has little customer contact. Luca's team is split into two factions, the result of his rumormongering and abysmal relations with the group's secretary—or so Hans believes. Hans doesn't particularly like Luca, who is very different from Hans: Luca is physically imposing, working class, a big spender who loves flashy cars and always seems to have money problems. Luca seems to feel similar antipathy toward Hans.

Although Luca's performance on the job isn't bad, Hans believes that Luca could achieve more, and improve overall group performance, if he spent less time gossiping and cultivated a better relationship with the secretary. He has casually mentioned this to Luca several times, to no avail, and Hans is ready to get rid of him. But from an informal poll of Luca's coworkers, Hans learns that most don't want him to go, despite the trouble he seems to cause. So Hans decides to confront Luca and demand that he get along with the secretary and stop playing office politics.

You may know firsthand the frustration that Hans feels: "I'm a reasonable person, trying to do a good job, facing an unreasonable person who refuses to acknowledge what is clearly the right and sensible way to solve this problem. I've told him what needs to be done. Why can't he *just do it?*" If you are faced with this situation, you're likely to simply give up, either by letting things drift or by firing the employee involved. Unfortunately, your moralizing stance and failure to realize that not everyone sees things the way you do will limit both your chances of successfully motivating the employee and the options you consider for solving the problem. You'll be better served if you let go of your desire to bring a bad employee to justice—and instead determine what can be gained by rehabilitating a wayward one. You will be more effective if you are willing to switch from your predetermined solution to an array of possible outcomes.

In the case here, Hans believes the solution is to change Luca's behavior, which he sees as the source of the team's turmoil and Luca's poor performance. But if Luca is to blame for the team's problems, why aren't his coworkers eager for him to go? Hans decides to gather more information to enrich his picture of the situation. He learns that the team's lack of customer contact may be depriving Luca of the stimulus he needs for job satisfaction. Just as important, it may be engendering a "rats in a cage" atmosphere for the entire back-office team—an environment of infighting further poisoned by a recently introduced financial incentive scheme and Hans's neglect of team-building initiatives.

Viewed this way, Luca's behavior may be the effect rather than the cause of the problem. Once Hans begins to think about what makes Luca tick, he wonders whether Luca's natural proclivity toward gossip and office politics might be channeled into a positive social endeavor such as team building. Sure, Luca needs to rebuild bridges with the secretary—not to mention with Hans—but the true motivational challenge may be to co-opt Luca as an ally to improve the entire office's climate.

Let's be clear: Reframing your goals in this way doesn't represent capitulation. Yes, you sometimes may settle on more modest and achievable goals for your problem employee, ones that the individual will get behind and is capable of meeting. But a willingness to be flexible in your aims can also yield novel and ambitious alternatives you may not have considered. In the end, you may not get exactly what you wanted from the employee, but you'll certainly get more than you did before.

Putting together a menu of possible outcomes is a crucial prerequisite to scheduling a formal encounter with the employee that is designed to solve or resolve the situation. Keep in mind that this menu may be augmented with a solution from that unlikeliest of sources: the employee. At the same time, this is not an "anything goes" agenda: You should be clear about bottom-line sticking points: those issues that, if you don't arrive at a solution to the problem, will shape a resolution—possibly the employee's termination.

Step 3: Stage the Encounter

Jerry has recently been appointed a department head at a pharmaceuticals company. As he settles in, he discovers he has inherited one very troublesome subordinate. Bernard—like Jerry, in his mid-30s—is an extremely competent scientist and very independent minded. Bernard performs well enough when given a defined

and highly complex piece of work that puts his technical expertise to the test. But he fails to discuss his
results until it is too late for Jerry to provide his own
input. And Bernard resists doing anything that departs
from his accustomed routines. Jerry suspects that
Bernard could do his work more quickly without sacrificing quality. But when Jerry raises the issue, Bernard
snows him with technical explanations that Jerry
doesn't fully understand.

Jerry learns that Bernard was once passed over for promotion and has had a bad attitude ever since. In fact,
Bernard has made it plain to everyone that he resents having to report to someone he regards as his inferior in technical knowledge. Although Jerry thinks that Bernard
should have been reined in long ago, he has attempted on
numerous occasions to win over Bernard with friendly
approaches. "What are you up to?" Jerry will ask. "You
always seem to have such a creative approach to problems." But Bernard rebuffs him: "You'll never understand
my work." Jerry is frustrated because he knows Bernard's
considerable skills are not being fully used to benefit the
business. And the growing animosity between the two
men doesn't bode well for improving the situation.

Hoping to help Bernard improve his performance,
Jerry has gone through the first step of the method presented here: piecing together a layered picture of the man
and how his past experiences and current situation (not
to mention Jerry's arrival) may have contributed to the
problem. Jerry decides that Bernard feels a need to preserve his dignity, which was diminished when he was
passed over for promotion. This trait is getting in the way
of Bernard making an energetic commitment to working
for Jerry. With this more nuanced understanding, Jerry
takes the method's second step: reevaluating what he

hopes to get out of Bernard. Jerry's own boss has advised him, as many bosses would, to assert his authority and tell Bernard to shape up or ship out. But Jerry knows that approach probably won't do much good. Instead, he hopes to motivate Bernard by leveraging his inherent desire for dignity, respect, and recognition. He would like Bernard to see that he is taking a self-defeating stance and that big personal rewards can be had from bringing these drives to bear on new challenges.

At the same time, Jerry knows he needs to be tougher than he has been. So he decides to undertake a focused, face-to-face encounter with Bernard. One positive by-product of Jerry's analysis of the situation is a certain detachment about Bernard: Jerry recognizes his own negative feelings—which have become increasingly intense in the face of Bernard's rudeness—but has put them aside before the encounter takes place. In fact, Jerry has even come to realize that he is part of the problem and that any positive outcome will almost assuredly require him to modify how he manages Bernard. If all goes well, Bernard, too, will begin to transform the way he views the situation.

This formal conversation with a problem employee, unlike the informal interactions you use to piece together a rich picture of the situation, is my method's third step. It should be a carefully staged event that underscores its importance. Hold the meeting on neutral ground—say, a conference room—and block out at least an hour for it. (In fact, it may take more than a single meeting, depending on how far you get in the first encounter.) You should tell the employee about it a day or so in advance, but emphasize that no materials or preparation are needed; this will not be a formal appraisal meeting but a chance to review and revise your working relationship. In fact, the only physical props you will need are a table and two chairs, set at a right angle.

The meeting opens with what I call an *affirmative assertion*, a brief "soft-hard" introduction. You affirm the employee's past and future value to the organization and express your desire for a mutually beneficial outcome to the meeting. But you also honestly describe the current problem as it looks to you and assert that things cannot and will not continue as they are now. For example, Jerry might say to Bernard:

"Thanks for meeting with me. I've been thinking about how we work together, and I have to tell you I'm not happy. My sense is that you aren't, either. I'm not exactly sure what the problem is. That's why I want us to talk now. I admire your talents and what you offer the company, but our previous conversations have shown me that we see our roles quite differently. I don't like the way you've responded to me on a number of occasions, but I realize you may feel the same way. I think you can help me to help us get on a different footing and identify new ways to work together. Certainly things can't go on the way they are—I won't let them."

You then need to engage in what I call *leverage questioning*. This is an intense and extended inquiry that tests hypotheses you have formulated in the course of developing your picture of the situation. Jerry's questions probe Bernard's need for recognition and ways in which it might be co-opted for productive ends. While one aim of such questions is to find unknown and potentially fruitful areas of agreement, they are also meant to bring differences into the open. In fact, one sign of a failed encounter—yet another "Sure, boss" meeting—is the employee managing to get out of the room without expressing a contrary view.

Care is needed here: It is very easy to slip back into telling and selling, shoveling facts and arguments onto the employee in order to bury that individual under the weight of the evidence. Even if you avoid this pitfall, the employee may still be evasive, defensive, hostile, or uncommunicative. Your goal is to discern in the haze of discontent the fleeting conversational windows that open up new views of the situation or offer opportunities to leverage your employee's driving passions.

For example, Jerry confronts Bernard on a sensitive issue: "Okay, I know you are technically superior to me. That's fine. So what do you think my role should be, then? What can I do to help you?"

Bernard doesn't hesitate in his response: "Nothing. Nobody around here with any technical smarts gets any respect anyway."

Jerry sees an opening: "Gee! Is that how you feel? Well, I guess I can see how that might have been a problem in the past. In fact, I understand why you were upset when you didn't get that promotion. But I value technical expertise. I think we could figure out how to put yours to better use—and in a way that would give you some credit for it."

The stage is set for the *moment of truth.* Jerry and Bernard have reached some agreement on at least part of the problem. And Jerry has brought Bernard to the point where he can help find a solution—one that plays to the qualities that motivate him. To return to the judo metaphor, Jerry has blocked Bernard by insisting that things will not continue as they are. Now Jerry will try to execute a throw, using Bernard's own energy as the impetus for movement toward Jerry's goals:

"Bernard. Thanks for being so open with me. I have a much better understanding of the issues as you see them.

What you are saying suggests that your job might be restructured so you can do things that take fuller advantage of your exceptional talents. I'm thinking, for example, of high-profile advisory and coaching work for teams within our unit. I'd like you to come up with some concrete proposals about what form this work might take. I'll do the same, and we'll meet again in a week. Listen, we'd rather keep you than lose you. But continuing in your present position, at least as you have defined it, is not viable. What do you think?"

The Broader Benefits

Remember that the method I have described guarantees a resolution, not a solution, to a problem of the kind Jerry faces. To see the difference between these two outcomes, let's return to Annette and Paolo. In her encounter with Colin, Annette engages in a new kind of conversation, hoping to figure out what his drivers are and where they are being blocked. She concludes that he is highly motivated in other areas of his life but doesn't respond well to pressure. She sees that such pressure will only be heightened if she tries to make him feel guilty about letting down his team when it needs him most. He needs different, not greater, responsibility. When Annette probes to find out what really engages Colin, the key turns out to be helping others. How can this insight be used to motivate him? During their meeting, Colin raises the possibility of assuming a training role—one that he successfully migrates into during the subsequent months.

Paolo's case is trickier and doesn't have such a happy ending. The problem is resolved but not solved. Paolo's original goal was to get George to admit that he needed to be more accountable for his work. But after some thinking, Paolo decides he simply wants George to see that moving beyond the current situation is going to require making some difficult choices. They sit down together and Paolo offers specific data about George's performance. These hard facts help George realize that he's having a problem in his new position and admit that he isn't motivated to solve it. The two agree that the next step is for Paolo to help George move into a role with less customer contact. This does indeed happen—but without Paolo's help. Two weeks after their meeting, George accepts a job with another company. While Annette got a clear win, Paolo had to console himself that the outcome was better than the collision he had expected: George being fired and taking his rage and resentment with him to another employer. In fact, George ultimately was probably grateful for the new beginning that sprang from his moment of truth with Paolo.

Whether a problem is solved or simply resolved, the payoffs to be gained by using this method extend beyond the present situation and the individuals involved. Besides increasing your chances of motivating problem individuals, the method can help you motivate your entire work group.

Turning around a problem person boosts everyone's morale. One of the most common workplace complaints is that bosses don't deal with poor performers. Typically, successive bosses leave a problem person alone, shying away from the mixture of cost and futility they anticipate would come from any attempt to improve matters. So when the employee perks up and starts acting more reasonably, the outward ripples are palpable.

But it's not just that people now find it easier working with someone who once was a problem. Your efforts also send a strong message. When people want a boss to "deal with" a poor performer, that doesn't always mean outright dismissal. Recall Luca's coworkers, who resisted Hans's efforts to sack the troublemaker. In your efforts to turn someone around—even if you ultimately fail and the person quits—people will see the mark of a manager and a culture that prefer problem solving to waste disposal. Summarily getting rid of someone, on the other hand, signals that the organization discards rather than deals with difficult people—and who knows who might be next?

The benefits across your organization can themselves justify the demands of this method. Yes, it can be time-consuming, difficult, and fraught with risks and setbacks: Although some employees may respond quickly to your approach, others might require time to rebuild positive relationships with you and their work. But at least they will be heading in the right direction, under their own steam. And in the end, you ideally will have not only a rehabilitated employee but also a healthier, more productive organization.

Decentering: The Art at the Heart of Motivation

THE CONCEPTUAL FOUNDATION of the motivational method presented here is the notion of "decentering." French child psychologist Jean Piaget coined the term to describe the phenomenon of infants moving beyond a state of locked-in, self-centered perception. This change enables them to understand that spatial perspectives different from their own are possible, that the person on the

other side of the table doesn't see the table the same
way. A similar shift in children's social perceptions—
understanding that people's values and motives may
also differ—comes later, especially when a child feels
some sympathy for the other person.

Adults aren't much different. With people we like, we
try to understand how they feel. But a lot of the time we
act in a kind of road rage: We're in the right, and others—abstract, disembodied, and barely real to us—are in
the wrong. Ask executives to talk about difficult subordinates—or even their own bosses—and you'll get adjec-
tives such as "lazy," "boring," and "dishonest," terms that
the employees or managers would never apply to themselves. Such blinkered perceptions, common in everyday
life, are particularly prevalent in the hierarchical setting of
business.

There's a certain comfort in keeping difficult people at
arm's length. By treating them as problems to be solved,
as objects to be manipulated with rewards and punish-
ments, we don't have to know what they think and feel.
That knowledge would only unsettle us. For example,
what if, in seeing things from their perspective, we saw
that our worldview wasn't necessarily the right one?

As a powerful aid to decentering, you should ask
yourself: "What must it be like for someone like that—that
is, with that character and perspectives—to have someone like me, with my biases and drives, as a boss, client,
subordinate?" The answer can guide your strategy for
future encounters.

Because of the effort it takes to decenter, particularly with difficult employees, the method I propose is
demanding. But it is no more difficult, and certainly
it is more effective, than motivational techniques based
on inspirational leadership. After all, can you really

inspire people you don't care for—and who aren't very fond of you?

Seven Hazards in Handling Problem People

The Mulberry Bush Chase. Have you been going round and round with someone, having the same fruitless conversations over and over? That's a sure sign of the need for a new approach. Discard your assumptions about the person and start afresh.

The Huckster Hazard. Have you been trying to "tell and sell"—that is, convince the person of the reasonableness of your position? Don't be an evangelist. Be a psychologist. The most successful salespeople discover and fulfill people's needs rather than try to change them.

The Ignorance-Is-Bliss Syndrome. Have you been contentedly clueless, neither knowing nor caring much about what makes an employee tick? You have to dig deeper to find out what drives that person—and what may be blocking those drivers.

The Self-Centeredness Trap. Do the words that spring to mind when you think about this person's behavior reflect a blinkered point of view? Ask yourself what words this individual would use to describe those same behaviors. It may give you a fresh insight into the nature of the problem.

The Hanging Judge Tendency. Have you been proudly occupying a moral high ground in your perspective on this person? It won't help to think of your employee as in the wrong while you act out the role of judge or high priest. Decide now whether you really want to solve the problem or sit in judgment.

The Monochrome Vision. Have you failed to search for any redeeming features in this person? Think hard. Because discovering even one positive characteristic in someone can color your relationship in entirely new ways and create a starting point for you to connect.

The Denial Danger. Have you been dismissing out of hand how someone perceives you? Remember the dictum, "If something is perceived as real, it is real in its consequences." It is the other person's reality you are going to have to work with, not just your own.

Originally published in January 2003
Reprint R0301D

One More Time: How Do You Motivate Employees?

FREDERICK HERZBERG

Executive Summary

IT'S A MANAGER'S PERENNIAL QUESTION: "How do I get an employee to do what I want?" The psychology of motivation is very complex, and what has been unraveled with any degree of assurance is small indeed. But the dismal ratio of knowledge to speculation has not dampened managers' enthusiasm for snake oil, new forms of which are constantly coming on the market, many of them with academic testimonials.

The surest way of getting someone to do something is to deliver a kick in the pants—put bluntly, the KITA. Because of the inelegance of a physical KITA and the danger that a manager might get kicked in return, companies usually resort to positive KITAs, ranging from fringe benefits to employee counseling. But while a KITA might produce some change in behavior, it doesn't motivate. Frederick Herzberg, whose work influenced a generation of scholars and managers, likens motivation to an internal generator. An employee with an internal generator, he argues, needs no KITA.

Achievement, recognition for achievement, the work itself, responsibility, and growth or advancement motivate people. The author cites research showing that those intrinsic factors are distinct from extrinsic, or KITA, elements that lead to job dissatisfaction, such as company administration, supervision, interpersonal relationships, working conditions, salary, status, and job security.

Managers tend to believe that job content is sacrosanct. But jobs *can* be changed and enriched. Managers should focus on positions where peoples' attitudes are poor, the investment needed in industrial engineering is cost-effective, and motivation will make a difference in performance.

When Frederick Herzberg researched the sources of employee motivation during the 1950s and 1960s, he discovered a dichotomy that stills intrigues (and baffles) managers: The things that make people satisfied and motivated on the job are different in kind from the things that make them dissatisfied.

Ask workers what makes them unhappy at work, and you'll hear about an annoying boss, a low salary, an uncomfortable work space, or stupid rules. Managed badly, environmental factors make people miserable, and they can certainly be demotivating. But even if managed brilliantly, they don't motivate anybody to work much harder or smarter. People are motivated, instead, by interesting work, challenge, and increasing responsibility. These intrinsic factors answer people's deep-seated need for growth and achievement.

Herzberg's work influenced a generation of scholars and managers—but his conclusions don't seem to have fully penetrated the American workplace, if the extraordinary attention still paid to compensation and incentive packages is any indication.

How many articles, books, speeches, and workshops have pleaded plaintively, "How do I get an employee to do what I want?"

The psychology of motivation is tremendously complex, and what has been unraveled with any degree of assurance is small indeed. But the dismal ratio of knowledge to speculation has not dampened the enthusiasm for new forms of snake oil that are constantly coming on the market, many of them with academic testimonials. Doubtless this article will have no depressing impact on the market for snake oil, but since the ideas expressed in it have been tested in many corporations and other organizations, it will help—I hope—to redress the imbalance in the aforementioned ratio.

"Motivating" with KITA

In lectures to industry on the problem, I have found that the audiences are usually anxious for quick and practical answers, so I will begin with a straightforward, practical formula for moving people.

What is the simplest, surest, and most direct way of getting someone to do something? Ask? But if the person responds that he or she does not want to do it, then that calls for psychological consultation to determine the reason for such obstinacy. Tell the person? The response shows that he or she does not understand you, and now an expert in communication methods has to be brought in to show you how to get through. Give the person a monetary incentive? I do not need to remind the reader of the complexity and difficulty involved in setting up and administering an incentive system. Show the person? This means a costly training program. We need a simple way.

Every audience contains the "direct action" manager who shouts, "Kick the person!" And this type of manager is right. The surest and least circumlocuted way of getting someone to do something is to administer a kick in the pants—to give what might be called the KITA.

There are various forms of KITA, and here are some of them:

NEGATIVE PHYSICAL KITA

This is a literal application of the term and was frequently used in the past. It has, however, three major drawbacks: 1) It is inelegant; 2) it contradicts the precious image of benevolence that most organizations cherish; and 3) since it is a physical attack, it directly stimulates the autonomic nervous system, and this often results in negative feedback—the employee may just kick you in return. These factors give rise to certain taboos against negative physical KITA.

In uncovering infinite sources of psychological vulnerabilities and the appropriate methods to play tunes on them, psychologists have come to the rescue of those who are no longer permitted to use negative physical KITA. "He took my rug away"; "I wonder what she meant by that"; "The boss is always going around me"—these symptomatic expressions of ego sores that have been rubbed raw are the result of application of:

NEGATIVE PSYCHOLOGICAL KITA

This has several advantages over negative physical KITA. First, the cruelty is not visible; the bleeding is internal and comes much later. Second, since it affects the higher cortical centers of the brain with its inhibitory powers, it reduces the possibility of physical backlash. Third, since the number of psychological pains that a person can feel is almost infinite, the direction and site possibilities of the KITA are increased many times. Fourth, the person administering the kick can manage to be above it all and let the system accomplish the dirty work. Fifth, those who practice it receive some ego satisfaction (one-upmanship), whereas they would find drawing blood abhorrent. Finally, if the employee does complain, he or she can always be accused of being paranoid; there is no tangible evidence of an actual attack.

Now, what does negative KITA accomplish? If I kick you in the rear (physically or psychologically), who is motivated? *I* am motivated; *you* move! Negative KITA does not lead to motivation, but to movement. So:

POSITIVE KITA

Let us consider motivation. If I say to you, "Do this for me or the company, and in return I will give you a reward, an incentive, more status, a promotion, all the quid pro quos that exist in the industrial organization," am I motivating you? The overwhelming opinion I receive from management people is, "Yes, this is motivation."

I have a year-old schnauzer. When it was a small puppy and I wanted it to move, I kicked it in the rear and it moved. Now that I have finished its obedience training, I hold up a dog biscuit when I want the schnauzer to move. In this instance, who is motivated—I or the dog? The dog wants the biscuit, but it is I who want it to move. Again, I am the one who is motivated, and the dog is the one who moves. In this instance all I did was apply KITA frontally; I exerted a pull instead of a push. When industry wishes to use such positive KITAs, it has available an incredible number and variety of dog biscuits (jelly beans for humans) to wave in front of employees to get them to jump.

Myths About Motivation

Why is KITA not motivation? If I kick my dog (from the front or the back), he will move. And when I want him to move again, what must I do? I must kick him again. Similarly, I can charge a person's battery, and then recharge it, and recharge it again. But it is only when one has a generator of one's own that we can talk about motivation. One then needs no outside stimulation. One *wants* to do it.

With this in mind, we can review some positive KITA personnel practices that were developed as attempts to instill "motivation":

1. REDUCING TIME SPENT AT WORK

This represents a marvelous way of motivating people to work—getting them off the job! We have reduced (formally and informally) the time spent on the job over the last 50 or 60 years until we are finally on the way to the "6 $^1/_2$-day weekend." An interesting variant of this approach is the development of off-hour recreation programs. The philosophy here seems to be that

Have spiraling wages motivated people? Yes, to seek the next wage increase.

those who play together, work together. The fact is that motivated people seek more hours of work, not fewer.

2. SPIRALING WAGES

Have these motivated people? Yes, to seek the next wage increase. Some medievalists still can be heard to say that a good depression will get employees moving. They feel that if rising wages don't or won't do the job, reducing them will.

3. FRINGE BENEFITS

Industry has outdone the most welfare-minded of welfare states in dispensing cradle-to-the-grave succor. One company I know of had an informal "fringe benefit of the month club" going for a while. The cost of fringe benefits in this country has reached approximately 25% of the wage dollar, and we still cry for motivation.

People spend less time working for more money and more security than ever before, and the trend cannot be reversed. These benefits are no longer rewards; they are rights. A 6-day week is inhuman, a 10-hour day is exploitation, extended medical coverage is a basic decency, and stock options are the salvation of American initiative. Unless the ante is continuously raised, the psychological reaction of employees is that the company is turning back the clock.

When industry began to realize that both the economic nerve and the lazy nerve of their employees had insatiable appetites, it started to listen to the behavioral scientists who, more out of a humanist tradition than from scientific study, criticized management for not knowing how to deal with people. The next KITA easily followed.

4. HUMAN RELATIONS TRAINING

More than 30 years of teaching and, in many instances, of practicing psychological approaches to handling people have resulted in costly human relations programs and, in the end, the same question: How do you motivate workers? Here, too, escalations have taken place. Thirty years ago it was necessary to request, "Please don't spit on the floor." Today the same admonition requires three "pleases" before the employee feels that a superior has demonstrated the psychologically proper attitude.

The failure of human relations training to produce motivation led to the conclusion that supervisors or managers themselves were not psychologically true to themselves in their practice of interpersonal decency. So an advanced form of human relations KITA, sensitivity training, was unfolded.

5. SENSITIVITY TRAINING

Do you really, really understand yourself? Do you really, really, really trust other people? Do you really, really, really, really cooperate? The failure of sensitivity training is now being explained, by those who have become opportunistic exploiters of the technique, as a failure to really (five times) conduct proper sensitivity training courses.

With the realization that there are only temporary gains from comfort and economic and interpersonal KITA, personnel managers concluded that the fault lay not in what they were doing, but in the employee's failure to appreciate what they were doing. This opened up the field of communications, a new area of "scientifically" sanctioned KITA.

6. COMMUNICATIONS

The professor of communications was invited to join the faculty of management training programs and help in making employees understand what management was doing for them. House organs, briefing sessions, supervisory instruction on the importance of communication, and all sorts of propaganda have proliferated until today there is even an International Council of Industrial Editors. But no motivation resulted, and the obvious thought occurred that perhaps management was not hearing what the employees were saying. That led to the next KITA.

7. TWO-WAY COMMUNICATION

Management ordered morale surveys, suggestion plans, and group participation programs. Then both management and employees were communicating and listening to each other more than ever, but without much improvement in motivation.

The behavioral scientists began to take another look at their conceptions and their data, and they took human relations one step further. A glimmer of truth was beginning to show through in the writings of the so-called higher-order-need psychologists. People, so they said, want to actualize themselves. Unfortunately, the "actualizing" psychologists got mixed up with the human relations psychologists, and a new KITA emerged.

8. JOB PARTICIPATION

Though it may not have been the theoretical intention, job participation often became a "give them the big picture" approach. For example, if a man is tightening 10,000 nuts a day on an assembly line with a torque wrench, tell him he is building a Chevrolet. Another approach had the goal of giving employees a "feeling" that they are determining, in some measure, what they do on the job. The goal was to provide a *sense* of achievement rather than a substantive achievement in the task. Real achievement, of course, requires a task that makes it possible.

But still there was no motivation. This led to the inevitable conclusion that the employees must be sick, and therefore to the next KITA.

9. EMPLOYEE COUNSELING

The initial use of this form of KITA in a systematic fashion can be credited to the Hawthorne experiment of the Western Electric Company during the early 1930s. At that time, it was found that the employees harbored irrational feelings that were interfering with the rational operation of the factory.

The opposite of job dissatisfaction is not job satisfaction, but no job dissatisfaction.

Counseling in this instance was a means of letting the employees unburden themselves by talking to someone about their problems. Although the counseling techniques were primitive, the program was large indeed.

The counseling approach suffered as a result of experiences during World War II, when the programs themselves were found to be interfering with the operation of the organizations; the counselors had forgotten their role of benevolent listeners and were attempting to do something about the problems that they heard about. Psychological counseling, however, has managed to survive the negative impact of World War II experiences and today is beginning to flourish with renewed sophistication. But, alas, many of these programs, like all the others, do not seem to have lessened the pressure of demands to find out how to motivate workers.

Since KITA results only in short-term movement, it is safe to predict that the cost of these programs will increase steadily and new varieties will be developed as old positive KITAs reach their satiation points.

Hygiene vs. Motivators

Let me rephrase the perennial question this way: How do you install a generator in an employee? A brief review of my motivation-hygiene theory of job attitudes is required before theoretical and practical suggestions can be offered. The theory was first drawn from an examination of events in the lives of engineers and accountants. At least 16 other investigations, using a wide variety of populations (including some in the Communist countries), have since been completed, making the original research one of the most replicated studies in the field of job attitudes.

The findings of these studies, along with corroboration from many other investigations using different procedures, suggest that the factors involved in producing job satisfaction (and motivation) are separate and distinct from the factors that lead to job dissatisfaction. (See the exhibit, which is further explained below.) Since separate factors need to be considered, depending on whether job satisfaction or job dissatisfaction is being examined, it follows that these two feelings are not opposites of each other. The opposite of job satisfaction is not job dissatisfaction but, rather, *no* job satisfaction; and similarly, the opposite of job dissatisfaction is not job satisfaction, but *no* job dissatisfaction.

Stating the concept presents a problem in semantics, for we normally think of satisfaction and dissatisfaction as opposites; i.e., what is not satisfying must be dissatisfying, and vice versa. But when it comes to understanding the behavior of people in their jobs, more than a play on words is involved.

Two different needs of human beings are involved here. One set of needs can be thought of as stemming from humankind's animal nature—the built-in drive to avoid pain from the environment, plus all the learned drives that become conditioned to the basic biological

Factors Affecting Job Attitudes as Reported in 12 Investigations

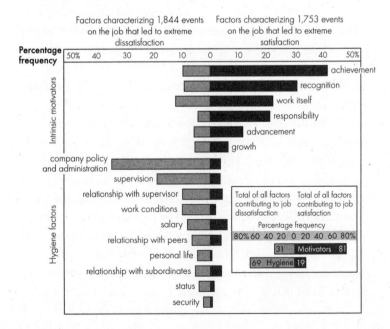

needs. For example, hunger, a basic biological drive, makes it necessary to earn money, and then money becomes a specific drive. The other set of needs relates to that unique human characteristic, the ability to achieve and, through achievement, to experience psychological growth. The stimuli for the growth needs are tasks that induce growth; in the industrial setting, they are the job content. Contrariwise, the stimuli inducing pain-avoidance behavior are found in the job environment.

The growth or *motivator* factors that are intrinsic to the job are: achievement, recognition for achievement, the work itself, responsibility, and growth or advance-ment. The dissatisfaction-avoidance or hygiene (KITA) factors that are extrinsic to the job include: company policy and administration, supervision, interpersonal relationships, working conditions, salary, status, and security.

A composite of the factors that are involved in caus-ing job satisfaction and job dissatisfaction, drawn from samples of 1,685 employees, is shown in the first exhibit. The results indicate that motivators were the primary cause of satisfaction, and hygiene factors the primary cause of unhappiness on the job. The employees, studied in 12 different investigations, included lower level super-visors, professional women, agricultural administrators, men about to retire from management positions, hospi-tal maintenance personnel, manufacturing supervisors, nurses, food handlers, military officers, engineers, scien-tists, housekeepers, teachers, technicians, female assem-blers, accountants, Finnish foremen, and Hungarian engineers.

They were asked what job events had occurred in their work that had led to extreme satisfaction or extreme dissatisfaction on their part. Their responses are broken down in the exhibit into percentages of total "positive" job events and of total "negative" job events. (The figures total more than 100% on both the "hygiene" and "motivators" sides because often at least two factors can be attributed to a single event; advancement, for instance, often accompanies assumption of responsibility.)

To illustrate, a typical response involving achievement that had a negative effect for the employee was, "I was unhappy because I didn't do the job successfully." A typical response in the small number of positive job events in the company policy and administration grouping was, "I was happy because the company reorganized the section so that I didn't report any longer to the guy I didn't get along with."

As the lower right-hand part of the exhibit shows, of all the factors contributing to job satisfaction, 81% were motivators. And of all the factors contributing to the employees' dissatisfaction over their work, 69% involved hygiene elements.

ETERNAL TRIANGLE

There are three general philosophies of personnel management. The first is based on organizational theory, the second on industrial engineering, and the third on behavioral science.

Organizational theorists believe that human needs are either so irrational or so varied and adjustable to specific situations that the major function of personnel management is to be as pragmatic as the occasion demands. If jobs are organized in a proper manner, they reason, the result will be the most efficient job structure, and the most favorable job attitudes will follow as a matter of course.

Industrial engineers hold that humankind is mechanistically oriented and economically motivated and that

human needs are best met by attuning the individual to
the most efficient work process. The goal of personnel
management therefore should be to concoct the most
appropriate incentive system and to design the specific
working conditions in a way that facilitates the most efficient use of the human machine. By structuring jobs in a
manner that leads to the most efficient operation, engineers believe that they can obtain the optimal organization of work and the proper work attitudes.

Behavioral scientists focus on group sentiments, attitudes of individual employees, and the organization's
social and psychological climate. This persuasion
emphasizes one or more of the various hygiene and motivator needs. Its approach to personnel management is
generally to emphasize some form of human relations
education, in the hope of instilling healthy employee attitudes and an organizational climate that is considered to
be felicitous to human values. The belief is that proper
attitudes will lead to efficient job and organizational
structure.

There is always a lively debate concerning the overall
effectiveness of the approaches of organizational theorists and industrial engineers. Manifestly, both have
achieved much. But the nagging question for behavioral scientists has been: What is the cost in human
problems that eventually cause more expense to the
organization—for instance, turnover, absenteeism,
errors, violation of safety

*In attempting to enrich
certain jobs, management
often reduces the
personal contribution of
employees rather than
giving them opportunities
for growth.*

rules, strikes, restriction of output, higher wages, and
greater fringe benefits? On the other hand, behavioral
scientists are hard put to document much manifest

improvement in personnel management, using their approach.

The motivation-hygiene theory suggests that work be *enriched* to bring about effective utilization of personnel. Such a systematic attempt to motivate employees by manipulating the motivator factors is just beginning. The term *job enrichment* describes this embryonic movement. An older term, job enlargement, should be avoided because it is associated with past failures stemming from a misunderstanding of the problem. Job enrichment provides the opportunity for the employee's psychological growth, while job enlargement merely makes a job structurally bigger. Since scientific job enrichment is very new, this article only suggests the principles and practical steps that have recently emerged from several successful experiments in industry.

JOB LOADING

In attempting to enrich certain jobs, management often reduces the personal contribution of employees rather than giving them opportunities for growth in their accustomed jobs. Such endeavors, which I shall call horizontal job loading (as opposed to vertical loading, or providing motivator factors), have been the problem of earlier job enlargement programs. Job loading merely enlarges the meaninglessness of the job. Some examples of this approach, and their effect, are:

- Challenging the employee by increasing the amount of production expected. If each tightens 10,000 bolts a day, see if each can tighten 20,000 bolts a day. The arithmetic involved shows that multiplying zero by zero still equals zero.

- Adding another meaningless task to the existing one, usually some routine clerical activity. The arithmetic here is adding zero to zero.

- Rotating the assignments of a number of jobs that need to be enriched. This means washing dishes for a while, then washing silverware. The arithmetic is substituting one zero for another zero.

- Removing the most difficult parts of the assignment in order to free the worker to accomplish more of the less challenging assignments. This traditional industrial engineering approach amounts to subtraction in the hope of accomplishing addition.

These are common forms of horizontal loading that frequently come up in preliminary brainstorming sessions of job enrichment. The principles of vertical loading have not all been worked out as yet, and they remain rather general, but I have furnished seven useful starting points for consideration in Exhibit 2.

A SUCCESSFUL APPLICATION

An example from a highly successful job enrichment experiment can illustrate the distinction between horizontal and vertical loading of a job. The subjects of this study were the stockholder correspondents employed by a very large corporation. Seemingly, the task required of these carefully selected and highly trained correspondents was quite complex and challenging. But almost all indexes of performance and job attitudes were low, and exit interviewing confirmed that the challenge of the job existed merely as words.

A job enrichment project was initiated in the form of an experiment with one group, designated as an achieving unit, having its job enriched by the principles described in the second exhibit. A control group continued to do its job in the traditional way. (There were also two "uncommitted" groups of correspondents formed to measure the so-called Hawthorne effect—that is, to gauge whether productivity and attitudes toward the job changed artificially merely because employees sensed that the company was paying more attention to them in doing something different or novel. The results for these groups were substantially the same as for the control

Principles of Vertical Job Loading

Principle	Motivators Involved
A. Removing some controls while retaining accountability	Responsibility and personal achievement
B. Increasing the accountability of individuals for own work	Responsibility and recognition
C. Giving a person a complete natural unit of work (module, division, area, and so on)	Responsibility, achievement, and recognition
D. Granting additional authority to employees in their activity; job freedom	Responsibility, achievement, and recognition
E. Making periodic reports directly available to the workers themselves rather than to supervisors	Internal recognition
F. Introducing new and more difficult tasks not previously handled	Growth and learning
G. Assigning individuals specific or specialized tasks, enabling them to become experts	Responsibility, growth, and advancement

group, and for the sake of simplicity I do not deal with them in this summary.) No changes in hygiene were introduced for either group other than those that would have been made anyway, such as normal pay increases.

The changes for the achieving unit were introduced in the first two months, averaging one per week of the seven motivators listed in the second exhibit. At the end of six months the members of the achieving unit were found to be outperforming their counterparts in the control group and, in addition, indicated a marked increase in their liking for their jobs. Other results showed that the achieving group had lower absenteeism and, subsequently, a much higher rate of promotion.

The third exhibit illustrates the changes in performance, measured in February and March, before the study period began, and at the end of each month of the study period. The shareholder service index represents quality of letters, including accuracy of information, and speed of response to stockholders' letters of inquiry. The index of a current month was averaged into the average of the two prior months, which means that improvement was harder to obtain if the indexes of the previous months were low. The "achievers" were performing less well before the six-month period started, and their performance service index continued to decline after the introduction of the motivators evidently because of uncertainty after their newly granted responsibilities. In the third month, however, performance improved, and soon the members of this group had reached a high level of accomplishment.

The fourth exhibit shows the two groups' attitudes toward their job, measured at the end of March, just before the first motivator was introduced, and again at the end of September. The correspondents were asked 16 questions, all involving motivation. A typical one was, "As you see it, how many opportunities do you feel that you have in your job for making worthwhile contributions?" The answers were scaled from 1 to 5, with 80 as the maximum possible score. The achievers became much more positive about their job, while the attitude of

Employee Performance in Company Experiment

Three-month cumulative average

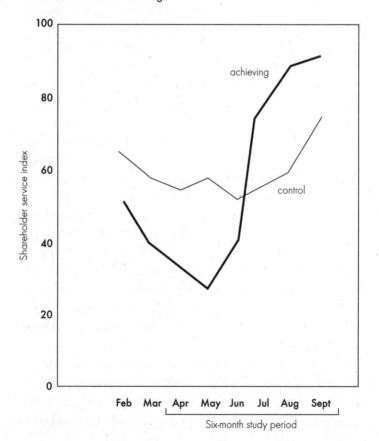

Six-month study period

the control unit remained about the same (the drop is not statistically significant).

How was the job of these correspondents restructured? The fifth exhibit lists the suggestions made that were deemed to be horizontal loading, and the actual vertical loading changes that were incorporated in the

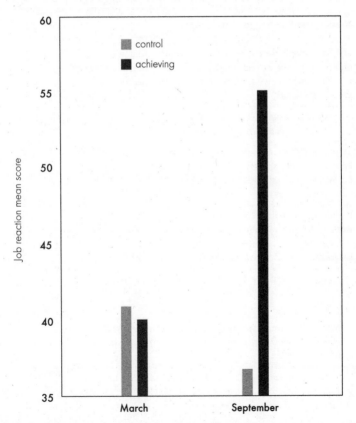

Change in Attitudes Toward Tasks in Company Experiment

Mean scores at beginning and end of six-month period

Enlargement vs. Enrichment of Correspondents' Tasks in Company Experiment

Horizontal Loading Suggestions Rejected

Firm quotas could be set for letters to be answered each day, using a rate that would be hard to reach.

The secretaries could type the letters themselves, as well as compose them, or take on any other clerical functions.

All difficult or complex inquiries could be channeled to a few secretaries so that the remainder could achieve high rates of output. These jobs could be exchanged from time to time.

The secretaries could be rotated through units handling different customers and then sent back to their own units.

Vertical Loading Suggestions Adopted	Principle
Subject matter experts were appointed within each unit for other members of the unit to consult before seeking supervisory help. (The supervisor had been answering all specialized and difficult questions.)	G
Correspondents signed their own names on letters. (The supervisor had been signing all letters.)	B
The work of the more experienced correspondents was proofread less frequently by supervisors and was done at the correspondents' desks, dropping verification from 100% to 10%. (Previously, all correspondents' letters had been checked by the supervisor.)	A
Production was discussed, but only in terms such as "a full day's work is expected." As time went on, this was no longer mentioned. (Before, the group had been constantly reminded of the number of letters that needed to be answered.)	D
Outgoing mail went directly to the mailroom without going over supervisors' desks. (The letters had always been routed through the supervisors.)	A
Correspondents were encouraged to answer letters in a more personalized way. (Reliance on the form-letter approach had been standard practice.)	C
Each correspondent was held personally responsible for the quality and accuracy of letters. (This responsibility had been the province of the supervisor and the verifier.)	B, E

job of the achieving unit. The capital letters under "Principle" after "Vertical Loading" refer to the corresponding letters in the second exhibit. The reader will note that the rejected forms of horizontal loading correspond closely to the list of common manifestations I mentioned earlier.

Steps for Job Enrichment

Now that the motivator idea has been described in practice, here are the steps that managers should take in instituting the principle with their employees:

1. Select those jobs in which a) the investment in industrial engineering does not make changes too costly, b) attitudes are poor, c) hygiene is becoming very costly, and d) motivation will make a difference in performance.

2. Approach these jobs with the conviction that they can be changed. Years of tradition have led managers to believe that job content is sacrosanct and the only scope of action that they have is in ways of stimulating people.

3. Brainstorm a list of changes that may enrich the jobs, without concern for their practicality.

4. Screen the list to eliminate suggestions that involve hygiene, rather than actual motivation.

5. Screen the list for generalities, such as "give them more responsibility," that are rarely followed in practice. This might seem obvious, but the motivator words have never left industry; the substance has just been rationalized and organized out. Words like "responsibility," "growth," "achievement," and "challenge," for example, have been elevated to the

lyrics of the patriotic anthem for all organizations. It is the old problem typified by the pledge of allegiance to the flag being more important than contributions to the country—of following the form, rather than the substance.

6. Screen the list to eliminate any *horizontal* loading suggestions.

7. Avoid direct participation by the employees whose jobs are to be enriched. Ideas they have expressed previously certainly constitute a valuable source for recommended changes, but their direct involvement contaminates the process with human relations *hygiene* and, more specifically, gives them only a *sense* of making a contribution. The job is to be changed, and it is the content that will produce the motivation, not attitudes about being involved or the challenge inherent in setting up a job. That process will be over shortly, and it is what the employees will be doing from then on that will determine their motivation. A sense of participation will result only in short-term movement.

8. In the initial attempts at job enrichment, set up a controlled experiment. At least two equivalent groups should be chosen, one an experimental unit in which the motivators are systematically intro-duced over a period of time, and the other one a con-trol group in which no changes are made. For both groups, hygiene should be allowed to follow its natu-ral course for the duration of the experiment. Pre- and post-installation tests of performance and job attitudes are necessary to evaluate the effectiveness of the job enrichment program. The attitude test

must be limited to motivator items in order to divorce employees' views of the jobs they are given from all the surrounding hygiene feelings that they might have.

9. Be prepared for a drop in performance in the experimental group the first few weeks. The changeover to a new job may lead to a temporary reduction in efficiency.

10. Expect your first-line supervisors to experience some anxiety and hostility over the changes you are making. The anxiety comes from their fear that the changes will result in poorer performance for their unit. Hostility will arise when the employees start assuming what the supervisors regard as their own responsibility for performance. The supervisor without checking duties to perform may then be left with little to do.

After successful experiment, however, the supervisors usually discover the supervisory and managerial functions they have neglected, or which were never theirs because all their time was given over to checking the work of their subordinates. For example, in the R&D division of one large chemical company I know of, the supervisors of the laboratory assistants were theoretically responsible for their training and evaluation. These functions, however, had come to be performed in a routine, unsubstantial fashion. After the job enrichment program, during which the supervisors were not merely passive observers of the assistants' performance, the supervisors actually were devoting their time to reviewing performance and administering thorough training.

What has been called an employee-centered style of supervision will come about not through education of supervisors, but by changing the jobs that they do.

JOB ENRICHMENT WILL NOT BE A one-time proposition, but a continuous management function. The initial changes should last for a very long period of time. There are a number of reasons for this:

- The changes should bring the job up to the level of challenge commensurate with the skill that was hired.

- Those who have still more ability eventually will be able to demonstrate it better and win promotion to higher level jobs.

- The very nature of motivators, as opposed to hygiene factors, is that they have a much longer-term effect on employees' attitudes. It is possible that the job will have to be enriched again, but this will not occur as frequently as the need for hygiene.

Not all jobs can be enriched, nor do all jobs need to be enriched. If only a small percentage of the time and money that is now devoted to hygiene, however, were given to job enrichment efforts, the return in human satisfaction and economic gain would be one of the largest dividends that industry and society have ever reaped through their efforts at better personnel management.

The very nature of motivators, as opposed to hygiene factors, is that they have a much longer-term effect on employees' attitudes.

The argument for job enrichment can be summed up quite simply: If you have employees on a job, use them. If you can't use them on the job, get rid of them, either via automation or by selecting someone with lesser ability. If you can't use them and you can't get rid of them, you will have a motivation problem.

Originally published in January 2003
Reprint R0301F

Management by Whose Objectives?

HARRY LEVINSON

IN THIS 1970 CLASSIC HBR ARTICLE, Levinson shares practical insights into the mysteries of motivation and takes a fresh look at the use and abuse of the most powerful tools for inspiring and guiding complex organizations. He argues that to motivate people successfully, management must focus on the question, "How do we meet both individual and organizational requirements?" When we make assumptions about individual motivations and increase pressure based on them, we ignore the fact that people work to meet their own psychological needs. Commitment must derive from the individual's wishes to support the organization's goals.

The performance appraisal systems that underpin MBO fail to take into account the deeper emotional components of motivation. Instead, managers are forced to commit to unrealistic goals. Superiors are profoundly uncomfortable rating people on performance, and they

execute this important task poorly. The individual's
desires are entirely absent from most performance measurement systems; managers assume that these desires
are perfectly aligned with corporate goals and that if
they're not, the individual should move on.

Self-motivation occurs when individual needs and
organizational requirements converge. However, successful management systems begin with the *employee's*
objectives. The manager's task is to understand the
employee's needs and then, with the employee, assess
how well the organization can meet them. Objectives
lack significant incentive power if they are unrelated to
employees' underlying personal aspirations. Management should give more weight to areas of discretion
open to the individual but not officially incorporated into
job descriptions or goals. Otherwise, a person may
objectively do an excellent job but still fail as a partner,
subordinate, superior, or colleague.

---

*At first glance this article seems to be about management
by objectives, an approach to performance appraisal
that's gone out of fashion for the most part. But read more
closely, it's an indictment of the measurement systems we
still use today. Harry Levinson, a gifted psychologist who
has published 13 articles in HBR, identified a constella-
tion of problems that cripple performance appraisal systems: Unit managers are forced to commit to goals they
don't believe are realistic. An obsession with objectivity
and quantitative measures means that quality is
neglected. Supervisors, who are profoundly uncomfortable
rating people on their performance, make a hash of this
critical task. Most important, in Levinson's view, the indi-*

*vidual's needs and desires are absent from the perfor-
mance measurement system; it's assumed that these are
in perfect alignment with corporate goals and that, if
they're not, the individual should move on.*

*Levinson's suggestions for reform recall Frederick
Herzberg's findings: People are most deeply motivated by
work that stretches and excites them while also advancing
organizational goals.*

D ESPITE THE FACT that the concept of management
by objectives (MBO) has by this time become an integral
part of the managerial process, the typical MBO effort
perpetuates and intensifies hostility, resentment, and
distrust between a manager and subordinates. As currently practiced, it is really just industrial engineering
with a new name, applied to higher managerial levels,
and with the same resistances intact.

Obviously, somewhere between the concept of MBO
and its implementation, something has seriously gone
wrong. Coupled with performance appraisal, the intent is
to follow the Frederick Taylor tradition of a more rational management process. That is, which people are to do
what, who is to have effective control over the process,
and how compensation is to be related directly to individual achievement. The MBO process, in its essence, is
an effort to be fair and reasonable, to predict performance and judge it more carefully, and presumably to
provide individuals with an opportunity to be self-
motivating by setting their own objectives.

The intent of clarifying job obligations and measuring
performance against an employee's own goals seems reasonable enough. The concern for having superior and
subordinate consider the same matters in reviewing the

performance of the latter is eminently sensible. The effort to come to common agreement on what constitutes the subordinate's job is highly desirable.

Yet, like most rationalizations in the Taylor tradition, MBO as a process is one of the greatest of managerial illusions because it fails to take adequately into account the deeper emotional components of motivation.

In this article, I shall indicate how I think management by objectives, as it is currently practiced in most organizations, is self-defeating and serves simply to increase pressure on the individual. By doing so, I am not rejecting either MBO or performance appraisal out of hand.

Rather, by raising the basic question, "Whose objectives?" I propose to suggest how they might be made into more constructive devices for effective management. The issues I shall raise have largely to do with psychological considerations, and particularly with the assumptions about motivation that underlie these techniques.

The "Ideal" Process

Because management by objectives is closely related to performance appraisal and review, I shall consider these together as one practice, which is intended:

- To measure and judge performance,

- To relate individual performance to organizational goals,

- To clarify both the job to be done and the expectations of accomplishment,

- To foster the increasing competence and growth of the subordinate,

- To enhance communications between superior and subordinate,

- To serve as a basis for judgments about salary and promotion,

- To stimulate the subordinate's motivation, and

- To serve as a device for organizational control and integration.

MAJOR PROBLEMS

According to contemporary thinking, the "ideal" process should proceed in five steps: 1) individual discussion with the superior of the subordinate's own job description, 2) establishment of the employee's short-term performance targets, 3) meetings with the superior to discuss the employee's progress toward targets, 4) establishment of checkpoints to measure progress, and 5) discussion between superior and subordinate at the end of a defined period to assess the results of the subordinate's efforts. In ideal practice, this process occurs against a background of more frequent, even day-to-day, contacts and is separate from salary review. But, in actual practice, there are many problems:

No matter how detailed the job description, it is essentially static—that is, a series of statements. However, the more complex the task and the more flexible an employee must be in it, the less any fixed statement of job elements will fit what that person does. Thus, the higher a person rises in an organization and the more varied and subtle the work, the more difficult it is to pin down objectives that represent more than a fraction of his or her effort.

With preestablished goals and descriptions, little weight can be given to the areas of discretion open to the individual but not incorporated into a job description or objectives. I am referring here to those spontaneously creative activities an innovative executive might choose to do, or those tasks a responsible executive sees need to be done. As we move toward a service society, in which tasks are less well defined but spontaneity of service and self-assumed responsibility are crucial, this becomes pressing.

Most job descriptions are limited to what employees do in their work. They do not adequately take into account the increasing interdependence of managerial work in organizations. This limitation becomes more important as the impact of social and organizational factors on individual performance becomes better understood. The more employees' effectiveness depends on what other people do, the less any one employee can be held responsible for the outcome of individual efforts.

If a primary concern in performance review is counseling the subordinate, appraisal should consider and take into account the total situation in which the superior and subordinate are operating. In addition, this should take into account the relationship of the subordinate's job to other jobs. In counseling, much of the focus is on helping the subordinate learn to negotiate the system. There is no provision in most reviews and no place on appraisal forms with which I am familiar to report and record such discussion.

The setting and evolution of objectives is done over too brief a period of time to provide for adequate interaction among different levels of an organization. This militates against opportunity for peers, both in the same work unit and in complementary units, to develop objectives together for maximum integration. Thus, both the setting of objectives and the appraisal of performance make little contribution to the development of teamwork and more effective organizational self-control.

The appraisal situation gives rise to powerful, paralyzing feelings of guilt that make it extremely difficult for most executives to be constructively critical of subordinates.

Coupled with these problems is the difficulty that superiors experience when they undertake appraisals. Douglas McGregor complained that the major reason appraisal failed was that superiors disliked playing God by making judgments about another person's worth.[1] He likened the superior's experience to inspection of assembly-line products and contended that his revulsion was against being inhuman. To cope with this problem, McGregor recommended that an individual should set his or her own goals, checking them out with the superior, and should use the appraisal session as a counseling device. Thus, the superior would become one who helped subordinates achieve their own goals instead of a dehumanized inspector of products.

Parenthetically, I doubt very much that the failure of appraisal stems from playing God or feeling inhuman. My own observation leads me to believe that managers experience their appraisal of others as a hostile, aggressive act that unconsciously is felt to be hurting or destroying the other person. The appraisal situation, therefore, gives rise to powerful, paralyzing feelings of guilt that make it extremely difficult for most executives to be constructively critical of subordinates.

OBJECTIVITY PLEA

Be that as it may, the more complex and difficult the appraisal process and the setting and evaluation of objectives, the more pressing the cry for objectivity. This is a vain plea. Every organization is a social system, a network of interpersonal relationships. A person may do an excellent job by objective standards of measurement, but may fail miserably as a partner, subordinate, superior, or colleague. It is a commonplace that more people fail to be promoted for personal reasons than for technical inadequacy.

Furthermore, because all subordinates are a component of their superiors' efforts to achieve their own goals, subordinates will inevitably be appraised on how well they work with superiors and help the latter meet goals. A heavy subjective element necessarily enters into every appraisal and goal-setting experience.

The plea for objectivity is made in vain for another reason. The greater the emphasis placed on measurement and quantification, the more likely the subtle, nonmeasurable elements of the task will be sacrificed. Quality of performance frequently, therefore, loses out to quantification.

A case example: One manufacturing plant that produces high-quality, high-prestige products, backed by a reputation for customer consideration and service, has instituted an MBO program. It is well worked out and has done much to clarify individual goals and organizational performance. It is an important component of the professional management style of that company, which has resulted in commendable growth.

But an interesting, and ultimately destructive, process has been set in motion. The managers are beginning to worry because now when they ask why something has not been done, they hear from one another, "That isn't in my goals." They complain that customer service is deteriorating. The vague goal, "improve customer service," is almost impossible to measure. There is therefore heavy concentration on those subgoals that can be measured. Thus, time per customer, number of customer calls, and similar measures are used as guides in judging performance. The less time per customer and the fewer the calls, the better the customer service manager meets his objectives. He is cutting costs, increasing profit—and killing the business. Worse still, he hates himself.

Most of the managers in that organization joined it because of its reputation for high quality and good service. They want to make good products and earn the continued admiration of their customers, as well as the envy of their industry. When they are not operating at that high level, they feel guilty. They become angry with themselves and the company. They feel that they might just as well be working for someplace else that admittedly does a sloppy job of quality control and could hardly care less about service.

The same problem exists with respect to the development of personnel, which is another vague goal that is hard to measure in comparison with subgoals that are measurable. If asked, each manager can name a younger employee as a potential successor, particularly if a promotion depends on doing so; but no one has the time, or indeed is being paid, to thoroughly train the younger person. Nor can one have the time or be paid, for there is no way in that organization to measure how well a manager does in developing another.

The Missed Point

All of the problems with objectives and appraisals outlined in the example discussed in the foregoing section indicate that MBO is not working well despite what some companies think about their programs. The underlying reason it is not working well is that it misses the whole human point.

To see how the point is being missed, let us follow the typical MBO process. Characteristically, top management sets its corporate goal for the coming year. This may be in terms of return on investment, sales, production, growth, or other measurable factors.

Within this frame of reference, reporting managers may then be asked how much their units intend to contribute toward meeting that goal, or they may be asked to set their own goals relatively independent of the corporate goal. If they are left free to set their own goals, these in any case are expected to be higher than those they had the previous year. Usually, each reporting manager's range of choices is limited to an option for a piece of the organizational action or improvement of specific statistics. In some cases, it may also include obtaining specific training or skills.

Once a reporting manager decides on the unit's goals and has them approved by his superior, those become the manager's goals. Presumably, he has committed himself to what he wants to do. He has said it and he is responsible for it. He is thereafter subject to being hoisted with his own petard.

Now, let us reexamine this process closely: The whole method is based on a short-term, egocentrically oriented perspective and an underlying reward-punishment psychology. The typical MBO process puts the reporting manager in much the same position as a rat in a maze, which has choices between only two alternatives. The experimenter who puts the rat in the maze assumes that the rat will choose the food reward. If that cannot be presumed, the rat is starved to make sure it wants the food.

Management by objectives differs only in that it permits the manager to determine his or her own bait from a limited range of choices. Having done so, the MBO process assumes that the manager will a) work hard to get it, b) be pushed internally by reason of this commitment, and c) be responsible to the organization for doing so.

In fairness to most managers, they certainly try, but not without increasing resentment and complaint for feeling like rats in a maze, guilt for not paying attention to those parts of the job not in their objectives, and passive resistance to the mounting pressure for ever-higher goals.

PERSONAL GOALS

The MBO process leaves out the answers to such questions as: What are the managers' personal objectives? What do they need and want out of their work? How do their needs and wants change from year to year? What relevance do organizational objectives and their part in them have to such needs and wants?

Obviously, no objectives will have significant incentive power if they are forced choices unrelated to a person's underlying dreams, wishes, and personal aspirations.

For example: If a salesperson relishes the pleasure of his relationships with his hard-earned but low-volume customers, this is a powerful need for him. Suppose his boss, who is concerned about increasing the volume of sales, urges him to concentrate on the larger-quantity customers rather than the smaller ones, which will provide the necessary increase in volume, and then asks him how much of an increase he can achieve.

To work with the larger-quantity customers means that he will be less likely to sell to the individuals with whom he has well-established relationships and be more likely to deal with purchasing agents, technical people, and staff specialists who will demand of him knowledge and information he may not have in sophisticated detail. Moreover, as a single salesperson, his organization may fail to support him with technical help to meet these demands.

When this happens, not only may he lose his favorite way of operating, which has well served his own needs, but he may have demands put on him that cause him to feel inadequate. If he is being compelled to make a choice about the percent of sales volume increase he expects to attain, he may well do that, but now he's under great psychological pressure. No one has recognized the psychological realities he faces, let alone helped him to work with them. It is simply assumed that because his sales goal is a rational one, he will see its rationality and pursue it.

The problem may be further compounded if, as is not unusual, formal changes are made in the organizational structure. If sales territories are shifted, if problems of delivery occur, if modes of compensation are changed, or whatever, all of these are factors beyond the salesperson's control. Nevertheless, even with certain allowances, he is still held responsible for meeting his sales goal.

PSYCHOLOGICAL NEEDS

Lest the reader think that the example we have just seen is overdrawn or irrelevant, I know of a young sales manager who is about to resign his job, despite success in it, because he chooses not to be expendable in an organization that he feels regards him only as an instrument for reaching a goal. Many young people are refusing to enter large organizations for just this reason.

Some may argue that my criticism is unfair, that many organizations start their planning and setting of objectives from below. Therefore, the company cannot be accused of putting a person in a maze. But it does so. In almost all cases, the only legitimate objectives to be set are those having to do with measurable increases in performance. This highlights, again, the question, "Whose objectives?" The question becomes more pressing in those circumstances where lower-level people set their objectives, only to be questioned by higher-level managers and told their targets are not high enough.

You may well ask, "What's the matter with that? Aren't we in business, and isn't the purpose of the employee's work to serve the requirements of the business?" The answer to both questions is, "Obviously." But that is only part of the story.

If a person's most powerful driving force is comprised of needs, wishes, and personal aspirations, combined with the compelling wish to look good in her own eyes for meeting those deeply held personal goals, then management by objectives should begin with *her* objectives. What does she want to do with her life? Where does she want to go? What will make her feel good about herself? What does she want to be able to look back on when she has expended her unrecoverable years?

At this point, some may say that those are her business. The company has other business, and it must assume that the employee is interested in working in the company's business rather than her own. That kind of differentiation is impossible. Everyone is always working toward meeting his or her psychological needs. Anyone who thinks otherwise, and who believes such powerful internal forces can be successfully disregarded or bought off for long, is deluded.

The Mutual Task

The organizational task becomes one of first understanding the employee's needs, and then, with him or her, assessing how well they can be met in this organization, doing what the organization needs to have done. Thus, the highest point of self-motivation arises when there is a complementary conjunction of the individual's needs and the organization's requirements. The requirements of both mesh, interrelate, and become synergistic. The energies of employee and organization are pooled for mutual advantage.

If the two sets of needs do not mesh, then a person has to fight him- or herself and the organization, in addition to the work that must be done and the targets that have been defined. In such a case, this requires the subordinate and the boss to evaluate together where the employee wants to go, where the organization is going, and how significant the discrepancy is. This person might well be better off somewhere else, and the organization would do better to have someone else in place whose needs mesh better with the organization's requirements.

LONG-RUN COSTS

The issue of meshed interests is particularly relevant for middle-aged, senior-level managers.[2] As people come into middle age, their values often begin to change, and they feel anew the pressure to accomplish many long-deferred dreams. When such wishes begin to stir, they begin to experience severe conflict.

Up to this point, they have committed themselves to the organization and have done sufficiently well in it to attain high rank. Usually, they are slated for even higher levels of responsibility. The organization has been good to them, and their superiors are depending on them to provide its leadership. They have been models for the younger employees, whom they have urged to aspire to organizational heights. To think of leaving is to desert both their superiors and their subordinates.

Because there are few avenues within the organization to talk about such conflict, these managers try to suppress their wishes. The internal pressure continues to mount until they finally make an impulsive break, surprising and dismaying both themselves and their colleagues. I can think of three vice presidents who have done just that.

The issue is not so much that they decide to leave, but the cost of the way they depart. Early discussion with superiors of their personal goals would have enabled both to examine possible relocation alternatives within the organization. If there were none, then both the managers and their superiors might have come to an earlier, more comfortable decision about separation. The organization would have had more time to make satisfactory alternative plans, as well as to have taken steps to compensate for the manager's lagging enthusiasm. Lower-level managers would then have seen the company as humane in its enlightened self-interest and would not have had to create fearful fantasies about what the top management conflicts were that had caused a good person to leave.

To place consideration of the managers' personal objectives first does not minimize the importance of the organization's goals. It does not mean there is anything wrong with the organization's need to increase its return on investment, its size, its productivity, or its other goals. However, I contend that it is ridiculous to make assumptions about the motivations of individuals, and then to set up means of increasing the pressures on people based on these often questionable assumptions. While there may be certain demonstrable short-run statistical gains, what are the long-run costs?

One cost is that people may leave; another, that they may fall back from competitive positions to plateaus. Why should an individual be expendable for someone else and sacrifice for something that is not a personal, cherished dream? Still another cost may be the loss of the essence of the business, as happened in the case example we saw earlier of the manufacturing plant with the problem of deteriorating customer service.

In that example, initially there was no dialogue. Nobody heard what the managers said, what they wanted, where they wanted to go, where they wanted the organization to go, and how they felt about the supposedly rational procedures that had been initiated. The underlying psychological assumption that management made unconsciously was that the managers had to be made more efficient; ergo, management by objectives.

Top management typically assumes that it alone has the prerogative to a) set the objectives, b) provide the rewards and targets, and c) drive anyone who works for the organization. As long as this reward-punishment psychology exists in any organization, the MBO appraisal process is certain to fail.

Many organizations are making this issue worse by promising young people they will have challenges because they assume these employees will be challenged by management's objectives. Managements are having difficulty, even when they have high turnover rates, hearing these youngsters say they could hardly care less for management's unilaterally determined objectives. Managements then become angry and complain that the young people do not want to work or that they want to become presidents overnight.

What the young people are asking is: What about me and my needs? Who will listen? How much will management help me meet my own requirements while also meeting its objectives?

The power of this force is reflected in the finding that the more a subordinate participates in the appraisal interview by presenting personal ideas and beliefs, the more likely he or she is to feel that a) the superior is helpful and constructive, b) some current job problems are being cleared up, and c) reasonable future goals are being set.[3]

Suggested Steps

Given the validity of all the MBO problems I have been discussing to this point, there are a number of possibilities for coping with them. Here, I suggest three beginning steps to consider.

MOTIVATIONAL ASSESSMENT

Every MBO program and its accompanying performance appraisal system should be examined as to the extent to which it a) expresses the conviction that people are patsies to be driven, urged, and manipulated, and b) fosters a genuine partnership between employee and organization, in which each has some influence over the other, as contrasted with a rat-in-maze relationship.

It is not easy for the nonpsychologist to answer such questions, but there are clues to the answers. One clue is how decisions about compensation, particularly bonuses, are made. For example: A sales manager asked for my judgment about an incentive plan for highly motivated salespeople who were in a seller's market. I asked why one was needed, and he responded, "To give them an incentive." When I pointed out that they were already highly motivated and apparently needed no incentive, he changed his rationale and said that the company wanted to share its success to keep the sales staff identified with it, and to express its recognition of their contribution.

I asked, "Why not let them establish the reward related to performance?" The question startled him; obviously, if they were going to decide, who needed him? A fundamental aspect of his role, as he saw it, was to drive them ever onward, whether they needed it or not.

In a plastic-fabricating company, a middle-management bonus plan tied to performance proved to be highly unsatisfactory. Frustrated that its well-intentioned efforts were not working and determined to follow precepts of participative management, ranking executives in the company involved many people in formulating a new one: personnel, control, marketing executives, and others—in fact, everyone but the managers who were supposed to receive the bonuses. Top management is now dismayed that the new plan is as unsatisfactory as the old and bitter that participation failed to work.

Another clue is the focus of company meetings. Some are devoted to intensifying the competition between units. Others lean heavily to exhortation and inspiration. Contrast these orientations with meetings in which people are apprised of problems and plan to cope with them.

GROUP ACTION

Every objectives and appraisal program should include group goal setting, group definition of individual and group tasks, group appraisal of its accomplishments, group appraisal of each individual member's contribution to the group effort (without basing compensation on that appraisal), and shared compensation based on the relative success with which group goals are achieved. Objectives should include long-term as well as short-term goals.

The rationale is simple. Every managerial job is an interdependent task. Managers have responsibilities to one another as well as to their superiors. The reason for having an organization is to achieve more together than each could alone. Why, then, emphasize and reward individual performance alone, based on static job descriptions? That approach can only orient people to incorrect and self-centered goals.

Therefore, where people are in complementary relationships, whether they report to the same superior or not, both horizontal and vertical goal formulation should be formalized, with regular, frequent opportunity for review of problems and progress. They should help one another define and describe their respective jobs, enhancing control and integration at the point of action.

In my judgment, for example, a group of managers (sales, promotion, advertising) reporting to a vice president of marketing should formulate their collective goals and define ways of helping one another and of assessing one another's effectiveness in the common task. The group assessment of each manager's work should be a means of providing each one with constructive feedback, not for determining pay. However, in addition to their salaries, they should each receive, as part of whatever additional compensation is offered, a return based on the group effort.

The group's discussion among itself and with its superior should include examination of organizational and environmental obstacles to goal achievement, and particularly of what organizational and leadership supports are required to attain objectives. One important reason for this is that often people think there are barriers where none would exist if they initiated action.

Every management by objectives and appraisal program should include regular appraisals of the manager by subordinates, and be reviewed by the manager's superior.

("You mean the president really wants us to get together and solve this problem?")

Another reason is that frequently when higher management sets goals, it is unaware of significant barriers to achievement, which makes managers cynical. For example, if there is no comprehensive orientation and support program to help new employees adapt, then pressure on lower-level managers to employ disadvantaged minority group members and to reduce their turnover can only be experienced by those managers as hollow mockery.

APPRAISAL OF APPRAISERS

Every management by objectives and appraisal program should include regular appraisals of the manager by subordinates, and be reviewed by the manager's superior. Every manager should be specifically compensated for how well he or she develops people, based on such appraisals. The very phrase "reporting to" reflects the fact that although a manager has a responsibility, the superior also has a responsibility for what he or she does and how it's done.

In fact, both common sense and research indicate that the single most significant outside influence on how a manager performs is the superior. If that is the case, then the key environmental factor in task accomplishment and managerial growth is the relationship between manager and superior.

Therefore, objectives should include not only the individual manager's personal and occupational goals, but also the corporate goals manager and superior share in common. They should together appraise their relationship vis-à-vis both the manager's individual goals and their joint objectives, review what they have done together, and discuss its implications for their next joint steps.

A manager rarely is in a position to judge a superior's overall performance, but he or she can appraise how well the superior has helped the manager to do the job, how well the superior is helping to increase the manager's proficiency and visibility, what problems the superior poses for the manager, and what kinds of support the superior can use. Such feedback serves several purposes.

Most important, it offers some guidance on the superior's own managerial performance. In addition, and particularly when the manager is protected by higher-level review of this appraisal, it provides the supervisor with direct feedback on his or her own behavior. This is much more constructive than behind-the-back complaints and vituperative terminal interviews, in which cases there is no opportunity either for self-defense or corrective behavior. Every professional counselor has had recently fired executive clients who did not know why they had been discharged for being poor superiors when, according to their information, their subordinates thought so much of them. In his or her own self-interest, every manager should want appraisal by subordinates.

The Basic Consideration

When the three organizational conditions we have just seen do in fact exist, then it is appropriate to think of starting management by objectives with a consideration of each employee's personal objectives; if the underlying attitude in the organization toward the subordinate is that he or she is but an object, there is certainly no point in starting with the person. Nor is there any point in trying to establish confidence in superiors when there is no protection from their rivalry, or being pitted against peers. Anyone who expressed personal fears and innermost wishes under these circumstances would be a damned fool.

The fundamental managerial consideration necessarily must be focused on the question: "How do we meet both individual and organizational purposes?"

For reasons I have already indicated, it should be entirely legitimate in every business for these concerns to be the basis for setting individual objectives. This is because the fundamental managerial consideration necessarily must be focused on the question: "How do we meet both individual and organizational purposes?" If a major intention of management by objectives is to enlist the self-motivated commitment of the individual, then that commitment must derive from the individual's powerful wishes to support the organization's goals; otherwise, the commitment will be incidental to any personal wishes.

Having said that, the real difficulty begins. How can any superior know what a subordinate's personal goals and wishes are if even the subordinate—as most of us are—is not clear about them? How ethical is it for a superior to pry into an employee's personal life? How can he or she keep from forming a negative judgment about someone who is losing interest in work, or is not altogether identified with the company? How can the superior keep that knowledge from interfering with judgments he or she might otherwise make, and opportunities he or she might otherwise offer? How often are the personal goals, particularly in middle age, temporary fantasies that are better not discussed? Can a superior who is untrained in psychology handle such information constructively? Will he or she perhaps do more harm than good?

These are critically important questions. They deserve careful thought. My answers should be taken as no more than beginning steps.

EGO CONCEPTS

Living is a process of constant adaptation. An individual's personal goals, wishes, and aspirations are continuously evolving and being continuously modified by experiences. That is one reason why it is so difficult for an individual to specify concrete personal objectives.

Nevertheless, each of us has a built-in road map, a picture of his or her future best self. Psychologists speak of this as an *ego ideal,* which is comprised of a person's values, the expectations parents and others have held out for competences and skills, and favorite ways of behaving. An ego ideal is essentially the way an individual thinks he or she ought to be. Much of a person's ego ideal is unconscious, which is another reason why it is not clear.

Subordinates' self-examination: Although people cannot usually spell out their ego ideal, they can talk about those experiences that have been highly gratifying, even exhilarating. They can specify those rare peak experiences that made them feel very good about themselves. When they have an opportunity to talk about what they have found especially gratifying and also what they think would be gratifying to them, people are touching on central elements of their ego ideal.

Given the opportunity to talk about such experiences and wishes on successive occasions, people can begin to spell out for themselves the central thrust of their lives. Reviewing all of the occupational choices they have made and the reasons for making them, people can begin to see the common threads in those choices and therefore the momentum of their personalities. As these become clearer, they are in a better position to weigh alternatives against the mainstream of their personalities.

For example, an individual who has successively chosen occupational alternatives in which she was individually competitive, and whose most exhilarating experiences have come from defeating an opponent or single-handedly vanquishing a problem, would be unlikely to find a staff position exhilarating, no matter what it paid or what it was called. Her ideal for herself is that of a vanquishing, competitive person.

The important concept here is that it is not necessary that an individual spell out concrete goals at any one point; rather, it is helpful to both the individual and the organization if he or she is able to examine and review aloud on a continuing basis personal thoughts and feelings in relation to his or her work. Such a process makes it legitimate to bring his or her own feelings to consciousness and talk about them in the business context as the basis for a relationship to the organization.

By listening, and helping the subordinate to spell out how and what he or she feels, the superior does not do anything to the subordinate, and therefore by that self-appraisal process cannot be hurtful. The information serves both employee and superior as a criterion for examining the relationship of the employee's feelings and, however dimly perceived, personal goals to organizational goals. Even if some of these wishes and aspirations are mere fantasy and impossible to gratify, if it is legitimate to talk about them without being laughed at, the individual can compare them with the realities of his or her life and make more reasonable choices.

Even in the safest organizational atmosphere, for reasons already mentioned, it will not be easy for managers to talk about their goals. The best-intentioned supervisor is likely to be something less than a highly skilled interviewer. These two facts suggest that any effort to ascertain a subordinate's personal goals is futile; but I think not.

The important point is not the specificity of the statement that any person can make, but the nature of a superior-subordinate relationship that makes it safe to explore such feelings and gives first consideration to the individual. In such a context, both subordinate and superior may come closer to evolving an employee-organization fit than they might otherwise.

Superior's introspection: An employee-organization relationship requires the superior to engage in some introspection, too. Suppose he has prided himself on bringing along a bright young manager who, he now learns, is thinking of moving into a different field. How can he keep from being angry and disappointed? How can he cope with the conflict he now faces when it is time to make recommendations for advancement or a raise?

The superior cannot keep from being angry and disappointed. Such feelings are natural in that circumstance. He can express feelings of disappointment to his protégé without being critical of the latter. But, if he continues to feel angry, then he needs to ask himself why another person's assertion of independence irritates him so. The issues of advancement and raises should continue to be based on the same realistic premises as they would have been before.

Of course, it now becomes appropriate to consider with the individual whether—in view of his feelings—he wants to take on the burden of added responsibility and can reasonably discharge it. If he thinks he does, and can, he is likely to pursue the new responsibility with added determination. With his occupational choice conflict no longer hidden, and with fewer feelings of guilt about it, his commitment to his chosen alternative is likely to be more intense.

And if an employee has earned a raise, he or she should get it. To withhold it merely punishes him or her, which puts the relationship back on a reward-punishment basis.

The question of how ethical it is to conduct such discussions as part of a business situation hinges on the climate of the organization and on the sense of personal responsibility of each executive. Where the organization's ethos is one of building trust and keeping confidences, there is no reason why executives cannot be as ethical as lawyers or physicians.

If the individual executive cannot be trusted in relationships with subordinates, then he or she cannot have their respect or confidence in any case, and the ordinary MBO appraisal process simply serves as a management pressure device. If the organization's ethos is one of rapacious internal competition, backbiting, and distrust, there is little point in talking about self-motivation, human needs, or commitment.

Management by objectives and performance appraisal processes, as typically practiced, are inherently self-defeating over the long run because they are based on a reward-punishment psychology that serves to intensify the pressure on the individual while really offering a very limited choice of objectives. Such processes can be improved by examining the psychological assumptions underlying them, by extending them to include group appraisal and appraisal of superiors by subordinates, and by considering the personal goals of the individual first. These practices require a high level of ethical standards and personal responsibility in the organization.

Such appraisal processes would diminish the feeling on the part of the superior that appraisal is a hostile, destructive act. While superior and subordinate would still have to judge the latter's individual performance, this judgment would occur in a context of continuing consideration for personal needs and reappraisal of organizational and environmental realities.

Not having to be continuously on the defensive and aware of the organization's genuine interest in having him or her meet personal as well as organizational goals, a manager would be freer to evaluate him- or herself against what has to be done. Because there would be many additional frames of reference in both horizontal and vertical goal setting, the manager would need no longer feel under appraisal, attack, or judgment as an isolated individual against the system. Furthermore, there would be multiple modes for contributing ideas and a varied method for exerting influence upward and horizontally.

In these contexts, too, the manager could raise questions and concerns about qualitative aspects of performance. Then manager, colleagues, and superiors could together act to cope with such issues without the barrier of having to consider only statistics. Thus, a continuing process of interchange would counteract the problem of the static job description and provide multiple avenues for feedback on performance and joint action.

In such an organizational climate, work relationships would then become dynamic networks for both personal and organizational achievements. A not-incidental gain from such arrangements is that problems would more likely be solved spontaneously at the lowest possible levels, and free superiors simultaneously from the burden of the passed buck and the onus of being the purveyors of hostility.

Notes

1. "An Uneasy Look at Performance Appraisal," HBR May–June 1957, p. 89. (Reprinted as an HBR Classic, September–October 1972.)

2. See my article, "On Being a Middle-Aged Manager," HBR July–August 1969, p. 51.

3. Ronald J. Burke and Douglas S. Wilcox, "Characteristics of Effective Employee Performance Reviews and Developmental Interviews," *Personal Psychology,* Vol. 22, No. 3, 1969, p. 291.

Originally published in January 2003
Reprint R0301H

Power Is the Great Motivator

DAVID C. MCCLELLAND AND

DAVID H. BURNHAM

Executive Summary

NOWADAYS, WITH ORGANIZATIONS growing ever
flatter and responsibility being pushed further down the
ranks, admitting to a desire for power is a little out of
fashion. But as the research in this 1976 classic HBR article shows, power is essential to good management.

In fact, when it comes to managing big companies, the
desire for power—that is, a manager's desire to have an
impact, to be strong and influential—is more important than
the need to get things done or the wish to be liked. The
need to achieve, while important in small companies,
actually becomes counterproductive in large, complex
organizations, leading managers to try to do things themselves rather than spread tasks among many people. And
managers who need to be liked tend to make exceptions
for particular subordinates' needs, undermining morale.
As their testimony reveals, other employees view those
exceptions as unfair.

But seeking power is not the same as seeking glory. People who want power only to further their own careers, rather than the goals of the organization, tend to have subordinates who are loyal to them but not to the company, making them less effective on the whole. And wanting power is not the same as throwing it around. Correlations between employee morale and sales figures show that individuals who manage by fiat are less effective than those whose style is more democratic.

If the research paints a complex picture of the role that power plays in good management, it also demonstrates how great the potential is for improvement once managers become familiar with their own motives and styles. As the many examples show, top executives can learn to tell who the good managers are likely to be and to train existing ones to be more effective.

Most HBR articles on motivation speak to managers about the people whose work they oversee. Curiously, the writers assume that the motivation of managers themselves—that is to say, of our readers—is so well aligned with organizational goals that it needs no examination. David McClelland and his colleague David Burnham knew better.

They found that managers fall into three motivational groups. Those in the first, affiliative managers, need to be liked more than they need to get things done. Their decisions are aimed at increasing their own popularity rather than promoting the goals of the organization. Managers motivated by the need to achieve—the second group— aren't worried about what people think of them. They focus on setting goals and reaching them, but they put their own achievement and recognition first. Those in the third group—institutional managers—are interested above all in power. Recognizing that you get things done inside organizations only if you can influence the people around you, they focus on building power through influence rather than through their own individual achievement. People in this third group are the most effective, and their direct reports have a greater sense of responsibility, see organizational goals more clearly, and exhibit more team spirit.

WHAT MAKES OR MOTIVATES a good manager? The question is enormous in scope. Some people might say that a good manager is one who is successful—and by now most business researchers and businesspeople know what motivates people who successfully run their own small businesses. The key to their success has turned out to be what psychologists call the need for achievement, the desire to do something better or more efficiently than it has been done before. Any number of books and articles summarize research studies explaining how the achievement motive is necessary for a person to attain success.

But what has achievement motivation got to do with good management? There is no reason on theoretical grounds why a person who has a strong need to be more efficient should make a good manager. While it sounds as if everyone ought to have the need to achieve, in fact, as psychologists define and measure achievement motivation, the need to achieve leads people to behave in ways that do not necessarily engender good management.

For one thing, because they focus on personal improvement, achievement-motivated people want to do things themselves. For another, they want concrete short-term feedback on their performance so that they can tell how well they are doing. Yet managers, particularly in large, complex organizations, cannot perform by themselves all the tasks necessary for success. They must manage others to perform for the organization. And they must be willing to do without immediate and personal feedback since tasks are spread among many people.

The manager's job seems to call more for someone who can influence people than for someone who does things better alone. In motivational terms, then, we might expect the successful manager to have a greater need for power than a need to achieve. But there must be other qualities besides the need for power that go into the makeup of a good manager. We will discuss here just what these qualities are and how they interrelate.

To measure the motivations of managers, we studied a number of individuals in different large U.S. corporations who were participating in management workshops designed to improve their managerial effectiveness. (See "Workshop Techniques" at the end of this article.) We concluded that the top manager of a company must possess a high need for power—that is, a concern for influencing people. However, this need must be disciplined and controlled so that it is directed toward the benefit of the institution as a whole and not toward the manager's personal aggrandizement. Moreover, the top manager's need for power ought to be greater than his or her need to be liked.

Measuring Managerial Effectiveness

What does it mean when we say that a good manager has a greater need for power than for achievement? Consider the case of Ken Briggs, a sales manager in a large U.S. corporation who joined one of our managerial workshops. (The names and details of all the cases that follow have been disguised.) About six years ago, Ken Briggs was promoted to a managerial position at headquarters, where he was responsible for salespeople who serviced his company's largest accounts.

In filling out his questionnaire at the workshop, Ken showed that he correctly perceived what his job required of him—namely, that he should influence others' success more than achieve new goals himself or socialize with his subordinates. However, when asked, with other members of the workshop, to write a story depicting a managerial situation, Ken unwittingly revealed through his fiction that he did not share those concerns. Indeed, he discovered that his need for achievement was very high—in fact, higher than the 90th percentile—and his need for power was very low, in about the 15th percentile. Ken's high need to achieve was no surprise—after all, he had been a very successful salesman—but obviously his desire to influence others was much less than his job required. Ken was a little disturbed but thought that perhaps the measuring instruments were not accurate and that the gap between the ideal and his score was not as great as it seemed.

Then came the real shocker. Ken's subordinates confirmed what his stories revealed: He *was* a poor manager, having little positive impact on those who worked for him. They felt that little responsibility had been delegated to them. He never rewarded them but only criticized them. And the office was poorly organized, confused, and chaotic. On all those scales, his office rated in the tenth to 15th percentile relative to national norms.

As Ken talked the results of the survey over privately with a workshop leader, he became more and more

upset. He finally agreed, however, that the results confirmed feelings he had been afraid to admit to himself or
others. For years, he had been miserable in his managerial role. He now knew the reason: He simply did not
want, and he had not been able, to influence or manage
others. As he thought back, he realized he had failed
every time he had tried to influence his staff, and he felt
worse than ever.

Ken had responded to failure by setting very high
standards—his office scored in the 98th percentile on
this scale—and by trying to do most things himself,
which was close to impossible. His own activity and lack
of delegation consequently left his staff demoralized.
Ken's experience is typical of those who have a strong
need to achieve but little desire for power. They may
become very successful salespeople and, as a consequence, may be promoted into managerial jobs for which
they, ironically, are unsuited.

If the need to achieve does not make a good manager,
what motive does? It is not enough to suspect that power
motivation may be important; one needs hard evidence
that people who are better managers than Ken Briggs is
are in fact more highly motivated by power and perhaps
score higher in other characteristics as well. But how
does one decide who is the better manager?

Real-world performance measures are hard to come
by if one is trying to rate managerial effectiveness in
production, marketing, finance, or research and development. In trying to determine who the better managers were in Ken Briggs's company, we did not want to
rely only on their superiors. For a variety of reasons,
superiors' judgments of their subordinates' real-world
performance may be inaccurate. In the absence of some
standard measure of performance, we decided that the

next best index of a manager's effectiveness would be the climate he or she creates in the office, reflected in the morale of subordinates.

Almost by definition, a good manager is one who, among other things, helps subordinates feel strong and responsible, rewards them properly for good performance, and sees that things are organized so that subordinates feel they know what they should be doing. Above all, managers should foster among subordinates a strong sense of team spirit, of pride in working as part of a team. If a manager creates and encourages this spirit, his or her subordinates certainly should perform better.

In the company Ken Briggs works for, we have direct evidence of a connection between morale and performance in the one area where performance measures are easy to find—namely, sales. In April 1973, at least three employees from each of this company's 16 sales districts filled out questionnaires that rated their office for organizational clarity and team spirit. Their scores were averaged and totaled to give an overall morale score for each office. Then, the percentage gains or losses in sales in 1973 were compared with those for 1972 for each district. The difference in sales figures by district ranged from a gain of nearly 30% to a loss of 8%, with a median gain of about 14%. The graph "The Link Between Morale and Sales" shows how, in Ken Briggs's company at least, high morale at the beginning of the year became a good index of how well the sales division would actually perform throughout the year. Moreover, it seems likely that the manager who can create high morale among salespeople can also do the same for employees in other areas (production, design, and so on), which leads to better overall performance. What characteristics, then, does a manager need to create that kind of morale?

The Power Factor

To find out, we surveyed more than 50 managers in both high- and low-morale units in all sections of a single large company. We found that the power motivation scores for most of the managers—more than 70%—were higher than those of the average person. This finding confirms that power motivation is important to management. (Remember that as we use the term, "power motivation" refers not to dictatorial behavior but to a desire to have an impact, to be strong and influential.) The better managers, as judged by the morale of those working

---

The Link Between Morale and Sales

The higher the morale early in the year, the higher the sales by year end.

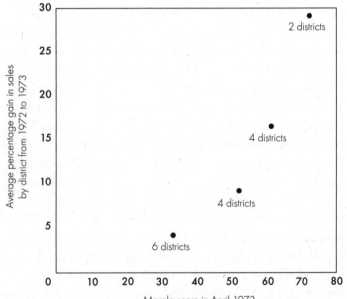

for them, tended to score even higher in power motivation. But the most important determining factor of high morale turned out to be not how their need for power compared with their need to achieve but whether it was higher than their need to be liked. This relationship existed for 80% of the better sales managers but for only 10% of the poorer managers. And the same held true for other managers in nearly every part of the organization.

In the research, product development, and operations divisions, 73% of the better managers had a stronger need for power than need to be liked, as compared with only 22% of the poorer managers, who tended to be what we term "affiliative managers"—whose strongest drive is to be liked. Why should this be so?

Sociologists have long argued that for a bureaucracy to function effectively, those who manage it must apply rules universally: that is, if they make exceptions for the particular needs of individuals, the whole system will break down. The manager with a high need to be liked is precisely the one who wants to stay on good terms with everybody and, therefore, is the one most likely to make exceptions for particular needs. If an employee asks for time off to stay home and look after a sick spouse and the kids, the affiliative manager agrees almost without thinking, out of compassion for the

Do our findings suggest that the good manager is one who cares for power and is not at all concerned about the needs of other people? Not quite.

employee's situation. When former President Gerald Ford remarked in pardoning Richard Nixon that Nixon had "suffered enough," he was responding as an affiliative manager would because he was empathizing primarily with Nixon's needs and feelings.

Sociological theory and our findings both argue, however, that the person whose need for affiliation is high does not make a good manager. This kind of person creates low morale because he or she does not understand that other people in the office will tend to regard exceptions to the rules as unfair to themselves, just as many U.S. citizens felt that it was unfair to let Nixon off and punish others who were less involved than he was in the Watergate scandal.

So far, our findings are a little alarming. Do they suggest that the good manager is one who cares for power and is not at all concerned about the needs of other people? Not quite, for the good manager has other characteristics that must still be taken into account. Above all, the good manager's power motivation is not oriented toward personal aggrandizement but toward the institution that he or she serves.

In another major research study, we found that the signs of controlled action, or inhibition, that appear when a person exercises imagination in writing stories tell a great deal about the kind of power that person needs.[1] We discovered that if a high power motivation score is balanced by high inhibition, stories about power tend to be altruistic. That is, the heroes in the story exercise power on behalf of someone else. This is the socialized face of power, as distinguished from the concern for personal power, which is characteristic of individuals whose stories are loaded with power imagery but show no sign of inhibition or self-control. In our earlier study, we found ample evidence that the latter individuals exercise their power impulsively. They are more often rude to other people, they drink too much, they try to exploit others sexually, and they collect symbols of personal prestige such as fancy cars or big offices.

Individuals high in power and in control, on the other hand, are more institution minded; they tend to get elected to more offices, to control their drinking, and to have a desire to serve others. Not surprisingly, we found in the workshops that the better managers in the corporation also tend to score high on both power and inhibition.

Three Kinds of Managers

Let us recapitulate what we have discussed so far and have illustrated with data from one company. The better managers we studied—what we call *institutional managers*—are high in power motivation, low in affiliation motivation, and high in inhibition. They care about institutional power and use it to stimulate their employees to be more productive. Now let us compare them with *affiliative managers* (those people for whom the need for affiliation is higher than the need for power) and with the *personal-power managers* (those in whom the need for power is higher than the need for affiliation but whose inhibition score is low).

In the sales division of the company we chose to use as an illustration, there are managers who match the three types fairly closely. The chart "Which Manager Is Most Effective?" shows how their subordinates rated the offices they worked in on responsibility, organizational clarity, and team spirit. Managers who are concerned about being liked tend to have subordinates who feel that they have little personal responsibility, believe that organizational procedures are not clear, and have little pride in their work group. In short, as we expected, affiliative managers make so many ad hominem and ad hoc decisions that they almost totally abandon orderly procedures. Their disregard for procedure leaves employees feeling weak, irresponsible, and without a sense of what might happen next, of where they stand in relation to their manager, or even of what they ought to be doing. In this company, the group of affiliative managers portrayed in the chart falls below the 40th percentile in all three measures of morale.

The managers who are motivated by a need for personal power are somewhat more effective. They are able to engender a greater sense of responsibility in their divisions and, above all, create a greater team spirit. They can be thought of as managerial equivalents of successful

---

Which Manager Is Most Effective?

Subordinates of managers with different motive profiles report different levels of responsibility, organizational clarity, and team spirit.

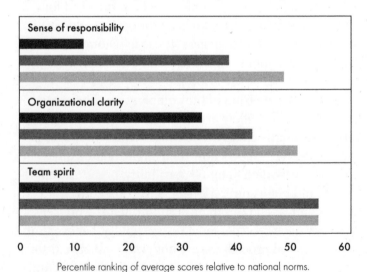

Sense of responsibility

Organizational clarity

Team spirit

0   10   20   30   40   50   60

Percentile ranking of average scores relative to national norms.

Scores for at least three subordinates of:
- ■ Affiliative managers (affiliation greater than power, high inhibition)
- ■ Personal-power managers (power greater than affiliation, low inhibition)
- ■ Institutional managers (power greater than affiliation, high inhibition)

tank commanders such as General George Patton, whose own daring inspired admiration in his troops. But notice how in the chart these people are still only around the 40th percentile in the amount of organizational clarity they create, whereas the institutional managers—the high-power, low-affiliation, high-inhibition managers—score much higher.

Managers motivated by personal power are not disciplined enough to be good institution builders, and often their subordinates are loyal to them as individuals rather than to the institution they serve. When a personal-power manager leaves, disorganization often follows. The strong group spirit that the manager has personally inspired deflates. The subordinates do not know what to do by themselves.

Of all the managerial types, the institutional manager is the most successful in creating an effective work climate. Subordinates feel that they have more responsibility. Also, those kinds of managers create high morale because they produce the greatest sense of organizational clarity and team spirit. If such a manager leaves, he or she can be more readily replaced by another because the employees have been encouraged to be loyal to the institution rather than to a particular person.

Since it seems undeniable that a manager with a power orientation creates better morale in subordinates than one with a people orientation, we must consider that a concern for power is essential to good management.

Our findings seem to fly in the face of a long and influential tradition of organizational psychology, which insists that authoritarian management is what is wrong with most businesses in the United States. Let us say frankly that we think the bogeyman of authoritarianism has been wrongly used to downplay the importance of power in management. After all, management is an

influence game. Some proponents of democratic management seem to have forgotten this fact, urging managers to be more concerned with people's personal needs
than with helping them to get things done.

But much of the apparent conflict between our findings and those of other behavioral scientists in this area
stems from the fact that we are talking about *motives,*
and behaviorists are often talking about *actions.* What
we are saying is that managers must be interested in
playing the influence game in a controlled way. That
does not necessarily mean that they are or should be
authoritarian in action. On the contrary, it appears that
power-motivated managers make their subordinates feel
strong rather than weak. The true authoritarian in action
would have the reverse effect, making people feel weak
and powerless.

Thus another important ingredient in the profile of a
manager is managerial style. In our example, 63% of the
better managers (those whose subordinates had higher
morale) scored higher on the democratic or coaching
styles of management as compared with only 22% of the
poorer managers. By contrast, the latter scored higher on
authoritarian or coercive management styles. Since the
better managers were also higher in power motivation, it
seems that in action they express their power motivation
in a democratic way, which is more likely to be effective.

To see how motivation and style interact, consider
the case of George Prentice, a manager in the sales
division of another company. George had exactly the
right combination of motives to be an institutional
manager. He was high in the need for power, low in the
need for affiliation, and high in inhibition. He exercised
his power in a controlled, organized way. The stories he
wrote reflected this fact. In one story, for instance, he
wrote, "The men sitting around the table were feeling

pretty good; they had just finished plans for reorganizing the company; the company has been beset with a number of organizational problems. This group, headed by a hard-driving, brilliant young executive, has completely reorganized the company structurally with new jobs and responsibilities. . . . "

This described how George himself was perceived by the company, and shortly after the workshop, he was promoted to vice president in charge of all sales. But George was also known to his colleagues as a monster, a tough guy who would "walk over his grandmother" if she stood in the way of his advancement. He had the right motive combination and, in fact, was more interested in institutional growth than he was in personal power, but his managerial style was all wrong. Taking his cue from some of the top executives in the corporation, he told people what they had to do, and he threatened them with dire consequences if they did not do it.

When George was confronted with his authoritarianism in a workshop, he recognized that this style was counterproductive—in fact, in another part of the study we found that it was associated with low morale—and he subsequently began to act more like a coach, which was the style for which he scored the lowest, initially. George saw more clearly that his job was not to force other people to do things but rather to help them figure out ways of getting their jobs done better for the company.

Profile of the Institutional Manager

One reason it was easy for George Prentice to change his managerial style was that, as we saw in his imaginative stories, he was already thinking about helping others—a characteristic of people with the institution-building motivational pattern. In further examining institution builders' thoughts and actions, we found they have four major characteristics:

- Institutional managers are more organization minded; that is, they tend to join more organizations and to feel responsible for building up those organizations. Furthermore, they believe strongly in the importance of centralized authority.

- They report that they like to work. This finding is particularly interesting because our research on achievement motivation has led many commentators to argue that achievement motivation promotes the Protestant work ethic. Almost the precise opposite is true. People who have a high need to achieve like to reduce their work by becoming more efficient. They would like to see the same result obtained in less time or with less effort. But managers who have a need for institutional power actually seem to like the discipline of work. It satisfies their need for getting things done in an orderly way.

- They seem quite willing to sacrifice some of their own self-interest for the welfare of the organization they serve.

- They have a keen sense of justice. It is almost as if they feel that people who work hard and sacrifice for the good of the organization should and will get a just reward for their effort.

It is easy to see how each of these four characteristics helps a person become a good manager, concerned about what the institution can achieve.

We discovered one more fact in studying the better managers at George Prentice's company. They were more mature. Mature people can be most simply described as less egotistic. Somehow their positive self-image is not at stake in their jobs. They are less defensive, more willing to seek advice from experts, and have a longer-range view. They accumulate fewer personal possessions and seem older and wiser. It is as if they have awakened to the fact that they are not going to live forever and have lost some of the feeling that their own personal future is all that important.

Many U.S. businesspeople fear this kind of maturity. They suspect that it will make them less hard driving, less expansion minded, and less committed to organizational effectiveness. Our data do not support their fears.

Those fears are exactly the ones George Prentice had before he went to the workshop. Afterward, he was a more effective manager, not despite his loss of some of the sense of his own importance but because of it. The reason is simple: His subordinates believed afterward that he was genuinely more concerned about the company than he was about himself. Whereas once they respected his confidence but feared him, they now trust him. Once, he supported their image of him as a "big man" by talking about the new Porsche and Honda he had bought; when we saw him recently, he said, almost as an aside, "I don't buy things anymore."

Altering Managerial Style

George Prentice was able to change his managerial style after learning more about himself. But does self-knowledge generally improve managerial behavior?

Consider the results shown in the chart "Managers *Can* Change Their Styles," where employee morale scores are compared before and after their managers attended workshop training. To judge by their subordinates' responses, the managers were clearly more effective after coming to terms with their styles. The subordinates felt that they received more rewards, that the organizational procedures were clearer, and that morale was higher.

But what do those differences mean in human terms? How did the managers change? Sometimes they decided they should get into another line of work. This happened to Ken Briggs, for example, who found that the reason he was doing so poorly as a manager was because he had almost no interest in influencing others. He understood how he would have to change in order to do well in his

Managers Can Change Their Styles

Training managers clearly improves their employees' morale.

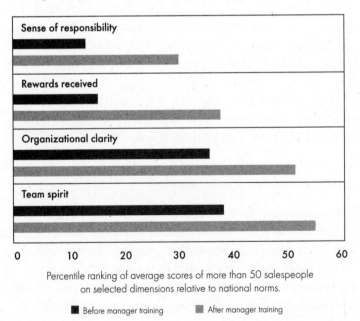

Percentile ranking of average scores of more than 50 salespeople on selected dimensions relative to national norms.

■ Before manager training   ▨ After manager training

present job but in the end decided, with the help of management, that he would prefer to work back into his first love, sales.

Ken Briggs moved into remaindering, helping retail outlets for his company's products get rid of last year's stock so that they could take on each year's new styles. He is very successful in this new role; he has cut costs, increased dollar volume, and in time worked himself into an independent role selling some of the old stock on his own in a way that is quite satisfactory to the business. And he does not have to manage anybody anymore.

In George Prentice's case, less change was needed. He obviously was a very competent manager with the right motive profile for a top company position. When he was promoted, he performed even more successfully than he had previously because he realized that he needed to become more positive in his approach and less coercive in his managerial style.

But what about a person who does not want to change jobs and discovers that he or she does not have the right motive profile to be a manager? The case of Charlie Blake is instructive. Charlie was as low in power motivation as Ken Briggs, his need to achieve was about average, and his affiliation motivation was above average. Thus he had the affiliative manager profile, and, as expected, the morale among his subordinates was very low. When Charlie learned that his subordinates' sense of responsibility and perception of a reward system were in the tenth percentile and that team spirit was in the 30th, he was shocked. When shown a film depicting three managerial climates, Charlie said he preferred what turned out to be the authoritarian climate. He became angry when the workshop trainer and other members in the group pointed out the limitations of this managerial style. He became obstructive to the group process, and he objected strenuously to what was being taught.

In an interview conducted much later, Charlie said, "I blew my cool. When I started yelling at you for being all wrong, I got even madder when you pointed out that, according to my style questionnaire, you bet that that was just what I did to my salespeople. Down underneath, I knew something must be wrong. The sales performance for my division wasn't so good. Most of it was due to me anyway and not to my salespeople. Obviously, their reports that they felt I delegated very little responsibility to them and didn't reward them at all had to mean something. So I finally decided to sit down and try to figure what I could do about it. I knew I had to start being a manager instead of trying to do everything myself and blowing my cool at others because they didn't do what I thought they should. In the end, after I calmed down, on the way back from the workshop, I realized that it is not so bad to make a mistake; it's bad not to learn from it."

After the course, Charlie put his plans into effect. Six months later, his subordinates were asked to rate him again. He attended a second workshop to study the results and reported, "On the way home, I was nervous. I knew I had been working with those guys and not selling so much myself, but I was afraid of what they would say about how things were going in the office. When I found out that the team spirit and some of those other low scores had jumped from around the 30th to the 55th percentile, I was so delighted and relieved that I couldn't say anything all day long."

When he was asked how his behavior had changed, Charlie said, "In previous years when corporate headquarters said we had to make 110% of our original goal, I had called the salespeople in and said, in effect, 'This is ridiculous; we are not going to make it, but you know perfectly well what will happen if we don't. So get out there and work your tails off.' The result was that I worked 20 hours a day, and they did nothing.

"This time I approached the salespeople differently. I told them three things. First, they were going to have to do some sacrificing for the company. Second, working harder is not going to do much good because we are already working about as hard as we can. What will be required are special deals and promotions. You are going to have to figure out some new angles if we are to make it. Third, I'm going to back you up. I'm going to set a realistic goal with each of you. If you make that goal but don't make the company goal, I'll see to it that you are not punished. But if you do make the company goal, I'll see to it that you will get some kind of special rewards."

The salespeople challenged Charlie, saying he did not have enough influence to give them rewards. Rather than becoming angry, Charlie promised rewards that were in his power to give—such as longer vacations.

Note that Charlie has now begun to behave in a number of ways that we found to be characteristic of the good institutional manager. He is, above all, higher in power motivation—the desire to influence his salespeople—and lower in his tendency to try to do everything himself. He asks people to sacrifice for the company. He does not defensively chew them out when they challenge him but tries to figure out what their needs are so that he can influence them. He realizes that his job is more one of strengthening and supporting his subordinates than of criticizing them. And he is keenly interested in giving them just rewards for their efforts.

The changes in his approach to his job have certainly paid off. The sales for his office in 1973 were more than

16% higher than those of the previous year, and they rose still further in 1974. In 1973, his office's gain over the previous year ranked seventh in the nation; in 1974, it ranked third. And he wasn't the only one in his company to change managerial styles. Overall sales at his company were up substantially in 1973, an increase that played a large part in turning the overall company performance around from a $15 million loss in 1972 to a $3 million profit in 1973. The company continued to improve its performance in 1974 with a further 11% gain in sales and a 38% increase in profits.

Of course, everybody can't always be reached by a workshop. Henry Carter managed a sales office for a company that had very low morale (around the 20th percentile) before he went for training. When morale was checked some six months later, it had not improved. Overall sales gains subsequently reflected this fact—only 2% above the previous year's figures.

Oddly enough, Henry's problem was that he was so well liked by everybody he felt little pressure to change. Always the life of the party, he was particularly popular because he supplied other managers with special hard-to-get brands of cigars and wines at a discount. He used his close ties with everyone to bolster his position in the company, even though it was known that his office did not perform as well as others.

His great interpersonal skills became evident at the workshop when he did very poorly at one of the business games. When the discussion turned to why he had done so badly and whether he acted that way on the job, two prestigious participants immediately sprang to his defense, explaining away Henry's failure by arguing that the way he did things was often a real help to others and the company. As a result, Henry did not have to cope with such questions at all. He had so successfully developed his role as a likable, helpful friend to everyone in management that, even though his salespeople performed badly, he did not feel under any pressure to change the way he managed people.

What have we learned from Ken Briggs, George Prentice, Charlie Blake, and Henry Carter? We have discovered what motives make an effective manager—and that change is possible if a person has the right combination of qualities.

Oddly enough, the good manager in a large company does not have a high need for achievement, as we define and measure that motive, although there must be plenty of that motive somewhere in his or her organization. The top managers shown here have a need for power greater than their interest in being liked. The manager's concern for power should be socialized—controlled so that the institution as a whole, not only the individual, benefits. People and nations with this motive profile are empire builders; they tend to create high morale and to expand the organizations they head. But there is also danger in this motive profile; as in countries, empire building can lead to imperialism and authoritarianism in companies. The same motive pattern that produces good power management can also lead a company to try to dominate others, ostensibly in the interests of organizational expansion. Thus it is not surprising that big business has had to be regulated periodically by federal agencies.

Similarly, the best managers possess two characteristics that act as regulators—a greater emotional maturity, where there is little egotism, and a democratic, coaching managerial style. If a manager's institutional power motivation is checked by maturity, it does not lead to an aggressive, egotistic expansiveness. That means managers can control their subordinates and influence others around them without having to resort to coercion or to an authoritarian management style.

Summarized in this way, what we have found out through empirical and statistical investigations may sound like good common sense. But it is more than common sense; now we can say objectively what the characteristics of the good manager are. Managers of corporations can select those who are likely to be good managers and train those already in managerial positions to be more effective with more confidence.

Workshop Techniques

WE DERIVED THE CASE STUDIES and data used in this article from a number of workshops we conducted, during which executives learned about their managerial styles and abilities, as well as how to change them. The workshops also provided an opportunity for us to study which motivation patterns in people make for the best managers.

At the workshops and in this article, we use the technical terms "need for achievement," "need for affiliation," and "need for power." The terms refer to measurable factors indicating motivation in groups and individuals. Briefly, those characteristics are measured by coding managers' spontaneous responses relating to how often they think about doing something better or more efficiently than before (need for achievement), about establishing or maintaining friendly relations with others (need for affiliation), or about having an impact on others (need for power). When we talk about power, we are not talking about dictatorial power but about the need to be strong and influential.

When the managers first arrived at the workshops, they were asked to fill out a questionnaire about their jobs. Each participant analyzed his or her job, explaining what he or she thought it required. The managers were asked to write a number of stories about pictures of various work situations we showed them. The stories were coded according to how concerned an individual was with achievement, affiliation, or power, as well as for the amount of inhibition or self-control they revealed. We then compared the results against national norms. The differences between a person's job requirements and his or her motivational patterns can often help assess whether the person is in the right job, is a candidate for promotion to another job, or is likely to be able to adjust to fit the present position.

To find out what kind of managerial style the participants had, we then gave them another questionnaire in which they had to choose how they would handle various realistic work situations in office settings. We divided their answers into six management styles, or ways of dealing with work situations. The styles were "democratic," "affiliative," "pacesetting," "coaching," "coercive," and "authoritarian." The managers were asked to comment on the effectiveness of each style and to name the style they preferred.

One way to determine how effective managers are is to ask the people who work for them. Thus, to isolate the characteristics that good managers have, we asked at least three subordinates of each manager at the workshop questions about their work situations that revealed

characteristics of their supervisors according to six criteria: 1) the amount of conformity to rules the supervisor
requires, 2) the amount of responsibility they feel they are
given, 3) the emphasis the department places on standards of performance, 4) the degree to which rewards
are given for good work compared with punishment
when something goes wrong, 5) the degree of organizational clarity in the office, and 6) its team spirit.[1] The managers who received the highest morale scores (organizational clarity plus team spirit) from their subordinates
were considered to be the best managers, possessing
the most desirable motive patterns.

We also surveyed the subordinates six months later to
see if morale scores rose after managers completed the
workshop.

We measured participants on one other characteristic deemed important for good management: maturity.
By coding the stories that the managers wrote, which
revealed their attitudes toward authority and the kinds of
emotions displayed over specific issues, we were able to
pinpoint managers at one of four stages in their progress
toward maturity. People in stage 1 are dependent on
others for guidance and strength. Those in stage 2 are
interested primarily in autonomy. In stage 3, people want
to manipulate others. In stage 4, they lose their egotistic
desires and wish to serve others selflessly.[2]

The conclusions we present in this article are based
on workshops attended by more than 500 managers
from some 25 U.S. corporations. We drew the examples
in the charts from one of those companies.

Notes

1. Based on George H. Litwin and Robert A. Stringer's Motivation and Organizational Climate (Harvard University Press, 1968).

2. Based on work by Abigail Stewart, as reported in David C. McClelland's Power: The Inner Experience (Irvington Publishers, 1979).

Notes

1. David C. McClelland, William N. Davis, Rudolf Kalin, and Eric Wanner, *The Drinking Man: Alcohol and Human Motivation* (Free Press, 1972).

Originally published in January 2003
Reprint R0301J

The Best-Laid Incentive Plans

STEVE KERR

Executive Summary

HIRAM PHILLIPS COULDN'T HAVE been in better spirits. The CFO and chief administrative officer of Rainbarrel Products, a diversified consumer-durables manufacturer, Phillips felt he'd single-handedly turned the company's performance around. He'd only been at Rainbarrel a year, but the company's numbers had, according to his measures, already improved by leaps and bounds.

Now the day had come for Hiram to share the positive results of his new performance management system with his colleagues. The corporate executive council was meeting, and even CEO Keith Randall was applauding the CFO's work: "Hiram's going to give us some very good news about cost reductions and operating efficiencies, all due to the changes he's designed and implemented this year." Everything looked positively rosy—until some questionable information began to trickle in from other meeting participants.

It came to light, for instance, that R&D had developed a breakthrough product that was not being brought to market as quickly as it should have been—thanks to Hiram's inflexible budgeting process. Then, too, an employee survey showed that workers were demoralized. And customers were complaining about Rainbarrel's service. The general message? The new performance metrics and incentives had indeed been affecting overall performance—but not for the better.

Should Rainbarrel revisit its approach to performance management? Commentators Steven Kaufman, a senior lecturer at Harvard Business School; compensation consultant Steven Gross; retired U.S. Navy vice admiral and management consultant Diego Hernández; and Barry Leskin, a consultant and former chief learning officer for Chevron Texaco, offer their advice in this fictional case study.

H<small>IRAM</small> <small>PHILLIPS</small> <small>FINISHED</small> tying his bow tie and glanced in the mirror. Frowning, he tugged on the left side, then caught sight of his watch in the mirror. Time to get going. Moments later, he was down the stairs, whistling cheerfully and heading toward the coffeemaker.

"You're in a good mood," his wife said, looking up from the newspaper and smiling. "What's that tune? 'Accentuate the Positive'?"

"Well done!" Hiram called out. "You know, I do believe you're picking up some pop culture in spite of yourself." It was a running joke with them. She was a classically trained cellist and on the board of the local symphony. He was the one with the Sinatra and Bing Crosby albums and the taste for standards. "You're getting better at naming that tune."

"Or else you're getting better at whistling." She looked over her reading glasses and met his eye. They let a beat pass before they said in unison: "Naaah." Then, with a wink, Hiram shrugged on his trench coat, grabbed his travel mug, and went out the door.

Fat and Happy

It was true. Hiram Phillips, CFO and chief administrative officer of Rainbarrel Products, a diversified consumer-durables manufacturer, was in a particularly good mood. He was heading into a breakfast meeting that would bring nothing but good news. Sally Hamilton and Frank Ormondy from Felding & Company would no doubt already be at the office when he arrived and would have with them the all-important numbers—the statistics that would demonstrate the positive results of the performance management system he'd put in place a year ago. Hiram had already seen many of the figures in bits and pieces. He'd retained the consultants to establish baselines on the metrics he wanted to watch and had seen various interim reports from them since. But today's meeting would be the impressive summation capping off a year's worth of effort. Merging into the congestion of Route 45, he thought about the upbeat presentation he would spend the rest of the morning preparing for tomorrow's meeting of the corporate executive council.

It was obvious enough what his introduction should be. He would start at the beginning—or, anyway, his own beginning at Rainbarrel Products a year ago. At the time, the company had just come off a couple of awful quarters. It wasn't alone. The sudden slowdown in consumer spending, after a decade-long boom, had taken the whole industry by surprise. But what had quickly become clear was that Rainbarrel was adjusting to the new reality far less rapidly than its biggest competitors.

Keith Randall, CEO of Rainbarrel, was known for being an inspiring leader who focused on innovation. Even outside the industry, he had a name as a marketing visionary. But over the course of the ten-year economic boom, he had allowed his organization to become a little lax.

Take corporate budgeting. Hiram still smiled when he recalled his first day of interviews with Rainbarrel's executives. It immediately became obvious that the place had no budget integrity whatsoever. One unit head had said outright, "Look, none of us fights very hard at budget time, because after three or four months, nobody looks at the budget anyway." Barely concealing his shock, Hiram asked how that could be; what did they look at, then? The answer was that they operated according to one simple rule: "If it's a good idea, we say yes to it. If it's a bad idea, we say no."

"And what happens," Hiram had pressed, "when you run out of money halfway through the year?" The fellow rubbed his chin and took a moment to think before answering. "I guess we've always run out of good ideas before we've run out of money." Unbelievable!

"Fat and happy" was how Hiram characterized Rainbarrel in a conversation with the headhunter who had recruited him. Of course, he wouldn't use those words in the CEC meeting. That would sound too disparaging. In fact, he'd quickly fallen in love with Rainbarrel and the opportunities it presented. Here was a company that had the potential for greatness but that was held back by a lack of discipline. It was like a racehorse that had the potential to be a Secretariat but lacked a structured training regimen. Or a Ferrari engine that needed the touch of an expert mechanic to get it back in trim. In other words, the only thing Rainbarrel was missing was what someone like Hiram Phillips could bring to the table. The allure was irresistible; this was the assignment that would define his career. And now, a year later, he was ready to declare a turnaround.

Lean and Mean

Sure enough, as Hiram steered toward the entrance to the parking garage, he saw Sally and Frank in a visitor parking space, pulling their bulky file bags out of the trunk of Sally's sedan. He caught up to them at the security checkpoint in the lobby and took a heavy satchel from Sally's hand.

Moments later, they were at a conference table, each of them poring over a copy of the consultants' spiral-bound report. "This is great," Hiram said. "I can hand this out just as it is. But what I want to do while you're here is to really nail down what the highlights are. I have the floor for 40 minutes, but I guess I'd better leave ten for questions. There's no way I can plow through all of this."

"If I were you," Sally advised, "I would lead off with the best numbers. I mean, none of them are bad. You hit practically every target. But some of these, where you even exceeded the stretch goal . . ."

Hiram glanced at the line Sally was underscoring with her fingernail. It was an impressive achievement: a reduction in labor costs. This had been one of the first moves he'd made, and he'd tried to do it gently. He came up with the idea of identifying the bottom quartile of performers throughout the company and offering them fairly generous buyout packages. But when that hadn't attracted enough takers, he'd gone the surer route. He imposed an across-the-board headcount reduction of 10% on all the units. In that round, the affected people were given no financial assistance beyond the normal severance.

"It made a big difference," he nodded. "But it wasn't exactly the world's most popular move." Hiram was well aware that a certain segment of the Rainbarrel workforce currently referred to him as "Fire 'em." He pointed to another number on the spreadsheet. "Now, that one tells a happier story: lower costs as a result of higher productivity."

"And better customer service to boot," Frank chimed in. They were talking about the transformation of Rainbarrel's call center—where phone representatives took orders and handled questions and complaints from both trade and retail customers. The spreadsheet indicated a dramatic uptick in productivity: The number of calls each service rep was handling per day had gone up 50%. A year earlier, reps were spending up to six minutes per call, whereas now the average was less than four minutes. "I guess you decided to go for that new automated switching system?" Frank asked.

As much as Rainbarrel liked to emphasize customer service in its values and mission statement, no reliable metric had been in place to track it.

"No!" Hiram answered. "That's the beauty of it. We got that improvement without any capital investment. You know what we did? We just announced the new targets, let everyone know we were going to monitor them, and put the names of the worst offenders on a great big 'wall of shame' right outside the cafeteria. Never underestimate the power of peer pressure!"

Sally, meanwhile, was already circling another banner achievement: an increase in on-time shipments. "You should talk about this, given that it's something that wasn't even being watched before you came."

It was true. As much as Rainbarrel liked to emphasize customer service in its values and mission statement, no reliable metric had been in place to track it. And getting a metric in place hadn't been as straightforward as it might seem—people haggled about what constituted "on time" and even what constituted "shipped." Finally, Hiram had put his foot down and insisted on the most objective of measures. On time meant when the goods were promised to ship. And nothing was counted as shipped till it left company property. Period. "And once again," Hiram announced, "not a dollar of capital expenditure. I simply let people know that, from now on, if they made commitments and didn't keep them, we'd have their number."

"Seems to have done the trick," Sally observed. "The percentage of goods shipped by promise date has gone up steadily for the last six months. It's now at 92%."

Scanning the report, Hiram noticed another huge percentage gain, but he couldn't recall what the acronym stood for. "What's this? Looks like a good one: a 50% cost reduction?"

Sally studied the item. "Oh, that. It's pretty small change, actually. Remember we separated out the commissions on sales to employees?" It came back to Hiram immediately. Rainbarrel had a policy that allowed current and retired employees to buy products at a substantial discount. But the salespeople who served them earned commissions based on the full retail value, not the actual price paid. So, in effect, employee purchases were jacking up the commission expenses. Hiram had created a new policy in which the commission reflected the actual purchase price. On its own, the change didn't amount to a lot, but it reminded Hiram of a larger point he wanted to make in his presentation: the importance of straightforward rules—and rewards—in driving superior performance.

"I know you guys don't have impact data for me, but I'm definitely going to talk about the changes to commission structure and sales incentives. There's no question they must be making a difference."

"Right," Sally nodded. "A classic case of 'keep it simple,' isn't it?" She turned to Frank to explain. "The old way they calculated commissions was by using this really complicated formula that factored in, I can't remember, at least five different things."

"Including sales, I hope?" Frank smirked.

"I'm still not sure!" Hiram answered. "No, seriously, sales were the most important single variable, but they also mixed in all kinds of targets around mentoring, prospecting new clients, even keeping the account information current. It was all way too subjective, and salespeople were getting very mixed signals. I just clarified the message so they don't have to wonder what they're getting paid for. Same with the sales contests. It's simple now: If you sell the most product in a given quarter, you win."

With Sally and Frank nodding enthusiastically, Hiram again looked down at the report. Row after row of numbers attested to Rainbarrel's improved performance. It wouldn't be easy to choose the rest of the highlights, but what a problem to have! He invited the consultants to weigh in again and leaned back to bask in the superlatives. And his smile grew wider.

Cause for Concern

The next morning, a well-rested Hiram Phillips strode into the building, flashed his ID badge at Charlie, the guard, and joined the throng in the lobby. In the crowd waiting for the elevator, he recognized two young women from Rainbarrel, lattes in hand and headphones around their necks. One was grimacing melodramatically as she turned to her friend. "I'm so dreading getting to my desk," she said. "Right when I was leaving last night, an e-mail showed up from the buyer at Sullivan. I just know it's going to be some big, hairy problem to sort out. I couldn't bring myself to open it, with the day I'd had. But I'm going to be sweating it today trying to respond by five o'clock. I can't rack up any more late responses, or my bonus is seriously history."

Her friend had slung her backpack onto the floor and was rooting through it, barely listening. But she glanced up to set her friend straight in the most casual way. "No, see, all they check is whether you responded to an e-mail within 24 hours of opening it. So that's the key. Just don't open it. You know, till you've got time to deal with it."

Then a belltone announced the arrival of the elevator, and they were gone.

More Cause for Concern

An hour later, Keith Randall was calling to order the quarterly meeting of the corporate executive council. First, he said, the group would hear the results of the

annual employee survey, courtesy of human resources
VP Lew Hart. Next would come a demonstration by the
chief marketing officer of a practice the CEO hoped to
incorporate into all future meetings. It was a "quick market intelligence," or QMI, scan, engaging a few of Rainbarrel's valued customers in a prearranged—but not
predigested—conference call, to collect raw data on customer service concerns and ideas. "And finally," Keith
concluded, "Hiram's going to give us some very good
news about cost reductions and operating efficiencies, all
due to the changes he's designed and implemented this
past year."

Hiram nodded to acknowledge the compliment. He
heard little of the next ten minutes' proceedings, thinking instead about how he should phrase certain points
for maximum effect. Lew Hart had lost him in the first
moments of his presentation on the "people survey" by
beginning with an overview of "purpose, methodology,
and historical trends." Deadly.

It was the phrase "mindlessly counting patents" that
finally turned Hiram's attention back to his colleague.
Lew, it seemed, was now into the "findings" section of his
remarks. Hiram pieced together that he was reporting on
an unprecedented level of negativity in the responses
from Rainbarrel's R&D department and was quoting the
complaints people had scribbled on their surveys.
"Another one put it this way," Lew said. "We're now
highly focused on who's getting the most patents, who's
getting the most copyrights, who's submitting the most
grant proposals, etc. But are we more creative? It's not
that simple."

"You know," Rainbarrel's chief counsel noted, "I have
thought lately that we're filing for a lot of patents for
products that will never be commercially viable."

"But the thing that's really got these guys frustrated seems to be their 'Innovation X' project," Lew continued. "They're all saying it's the best thing since sliced bread, a generational leap on the product line, but they're getting no uptake."

Eyes in the room turned to the products division president, who promptly threw up his hands. "What can I say, gang? We never expected that breakthrough to happen in this fiscal year. It's not in the budget to bring it to market."

Lew Hart silenced the rising voices, reminding the group he had more findings to share. Unfortunately, it didn't get much better. Both current and retired employees were complaining about being treated poorly by sales personnel when they sought to place orders or obtain information about company products. There was a lot of residual unhappiness about the layoffs, and not simply because those who remained had more work to do. Some people had noted that, because the reduction was based on headcount, not costs, managers had tended to fire low-level people, crippling the company without saving much money. And because the reduction was across the board, the highest performing departments had been forced to lay off some of the company's best employees. Others had heard about inequities in the severance deals: "As far as I can tell, we gave our lowest performers a better package than our good ones," he quoted one employee as saying.

And then there was a chorus of complaints from the sales organization. "No role models." "No mentoring." "No chance to pick the veterans' brains." "No knowledge sharing about accounts." More than ever, salespeople were dissatisfied with their territories and clamoring for the more affluent, high-volume districts. "It didn't help that all the sales-contest winners this year were from places like Scarsdale, Shaker Heights, and Beverly Hills," a salesperson was quoted as saying. Lew concluded with a promise to look further into the apparent decline in morale to determine whether it was an aberration.

The Ugly Truth

But if the group thought the mood would improve in the meeting's next segment—the QMI chat with the folks at longtime customer Brenton Brothers—they soon found out otherwise. Booming out of the speakerphone in the middle of the table came the Southern-tinged voices of Billy Brenton and three of his employees representing various parts of his organization.

"What's up with your shipping department?" Billy called out. "My people are telling me it's taking forever to get the stock replenished."

Hiram sat up straight, then leaned toward the speakerphone. "Excuse me, Mr. Brenton. This is Hiram Phillips—I don't believe we've met. But are you saying we are not shipping by our promise date?"

A cough—or was it a guffaw?—came back across the wire. "Well, son. Let me tell you about that. First of all, what y'all promise is not always what we are saying we require—and what we believe we deserve. Annie, isn't that right?"

"Yes, Mr. Brenton," said the buyer. "In some cases, I've been told to take a late date or otherwise forgo the purchase. That becomes the promise date, I guess, but it's not the date I asked for."

"And second," Billy continued, "I can't figure out how you fellas define 'shipped.' We were told last Tuesday an order had been shipped, and come to find out, the stuff was sitting on a railroad siding across the street from your plant."

"That's an important order for us," another Brenton voice piped up. "I sent an e-mail to try to sort it out, but I haven't heard back about it." Hiram winced, recalling the conversation in the lobby that morning. The voice persisted: "I thought that might be the better way to contact your service people these days? They always seem in such an all-fired hurry to get off the phone when I call. Sometimes it takes two or three calls to get something squared away."

"I can't figure out how you fellas define 'shipped.' We were told last Tuesday an order had been shipped, and come to find out, the stuff was sitting on a railroad siding across the street from your plant."

The call didn't end there—a few more shortcomings were discussed. Then Keith Randall, to his credit, pulled the conversation onto more positive ground by reaffirming the great regard Rainbarrel had for Brenton Brothers and the mutual value of that enduring relationship. Promises were made and hearty thanks extended for the frank feedback. Meanwhile, Hiram felt the eyes of his colleagues on him. Finally, the call ended and the CEO announced that he, for one, needed a break before the last agenda item.

Dazed and Confused

Hiram considered following his boss out of the room and asking him to table the whole discussion of the new metrics and incentives. The climate was suddenly bad for the news he had looked forward to sharing. But he knew that delaying the discussion would be weak and wrong. After all, he had plenty of evidence to show he was on the right track. The problems the group had just been hearing about were side effects, but surely they didn't outweigh the cure.

He moved to the side table and poured a glass of ice water, then leaned against the wall to collect his thoughts. Perhaps he should reframe his opening comments in light of the employee and customer feedback. As he considered how he might do so, Keith Randall appeared at his side.

"Looks like we have our work cut out for us, eh Hiram?" he said quietly—and charitably enough. "Some of those metrics taking hold, um, a little too strongly?" Hiram started to object but saw the seriousness in his boss's eyes.

He lifted the stack of reports Felding & Company had prepared for him and turned to the conference table. "Well, I guess that's something for the group to talk about."

Should Rainbarrel revisit its approach to performance management?

Four commentators offer expert advice.

STEPHEN P. KAUFMAN *recently retired as chairman of the board of Arrow Electronics, a company he served as CEO for 14 years. He is a senior lecturer at Harvard Business School in Boston.*

If Rainbarrel were within a month of bankruptcy and in the hands of a turnaround manager, the kinds of changes Hiram has imposed wouldn't be so unusual and might even be considered reasonable. But as far as I can tell, Rainbarrel just needs to tighten its belt in a period of cyclically soft sales and more aggressive competition. The case portrays Rainbarrel Products as a basically healthy and successful company.

But I'd bet that we as readers are seeing only half the trouble Hiram has caused. Given the pressure to ship faster, the warehouse is probably making more errors and thus adding to the number of returns and customer complaints. Now that every department has cut its staff, the company is probably hiring more expensive temps, consultants, and outsourcing firms. And let's not even speculate on what the impact of a "wall of shame" might be. That's the kind of humiliating tactic that could turn a devoted employee into a saboteur.

These troubles should be enough to teach Rainbarrel the first rule of performance management: You get what you pay for. If the warehouse workers are praised for putting a box over an imaginary line, they will put it there even if it's not ready. If you pay the sales force only for sales dollars, you might end up with more sales, but at bad prices or with too many extra services promised. I remember a time at Arrow Electronics when we decided to pay out a part of the sales reps' commissions at the time they took the customers' orders. The result was that we got orders that never shipped—or that were shipped and later returned for full credit. One veteran salesman explained it this way, and I've heard the phrase many times since: "Look, you make the rules, we'll play the game."

It's very difficult to define the right metric and anticipate exactly how your people will react to it. Your best chance of knowing whether it will have the intended effect is to talk to the people directly involved.

Before top management starts introducing new rules, then, it had better have a good sense of the kinds of games these rules may promote. Hiram is blindsided by the discovery that his customer service people have learned not to open problematic e-mails. I made a similar mistake years ago by requiring Arrow warehouses to ship all orders received by 4 PM the same day. Since the orders were routed by our computer to a printer in the warehouse, the key to 100% same-day shipping performance was obvious: They pulled the plug on the printer at three o'clock.

All of this suggests another truism about performance management: The devil is in the details. It's very difficult to define the right metric and anticipate exactly how your people will react to it. Your best chance of knowing whether it will have the intended effect is to talk to the people directly involved as well as their immediate supervisors. It's very telling that Hiram is seen meeting with only his henchmen. He needs to go to the cafeteria, get a tray, and sit with the people who are doing the work at Rainbarrel. If he were my new chief financial officer, I'd have told him, "Staple yourself to the back of a warehouse manager for a week. Take the time to follow a general manager around his division. Ride along with some salespeople. Spend several months getting to know this company really well before you settle into your staff job." Hiram knows nothing about Rainbarrel's industry and how it works and knows little or nothing about the culture of the company. He must understand both in order to know what kind and what pace of change are appropriate in this situation.

That point brings me to a big question about the Rainbarrel case. Where has the CEO been? Keith Randall has seriously abdicated his responsibilities as chief executive in giving a newly hired CFO such free rein—and across such a broad range of functions, many of them typically not a CFO's job. When I was a young man, my father told me, "Good judgment comes from experience. But unfortunately, experience comes from bad judgment." A manager's career is all about building a base of good judgment on the back of mistakes. Hiram, if he's at all reflective, will learn a lesson here. But his boss should have known it by now.

STEVEN E. GROSS *leads the U.S. compensation consulting practice of Mercer Human Resource Consulting. Based in Philadelphia, he is a frequent author and speaker on reward issues.*

The good news in this case is that we see a senior management team that is focusing on performance measures as a way of creating more accountability for results. The bad news is that the team is using the wrong measures, and it has gone about establishing them in the wrong way. As a result, it is sacrificing long-term business success for short-term operational gains. What Rainbarrel needs are performance metrics that are less employee focused and more customer focused. But even these kinds of externally focused measures are likely to be ineffective unless management can successfully help workers understand and accept them.

Many of Hiram's metrics were based on the assumption that the organization wasn't working hard enough, but that's usually not the case in most companies.

The only reasonable way to embark on any performance management effort is to define the criteria for
success, and that's a step Hiram seems to have skipped.
What's the ultimate goal? Sales? Profits? Retained business? Lacking that big picture, Hiram is focusing on
intermediary steps and assuming that such enhance-
ments will produce a positive impact on the bottom line.
Measuring the number of calls being handled by the call
center is a good example. That's a customer service measure but not an indicator of customer satisfaction. "Did
one call solve the customer's problem?" might be a better
question for them to ask. Employee turnover is another
metric that might make sense, given that employee
tenure is highly correlated to the quality of customer service in these kinds of jobs. Practically speaking, it's
always tricky to balance what can be measured objectively and internally, what customers really want, and
what ultimately creates value for the organization.

If I were Hiram, I wouldn't have made a single change
until I'd asked two basic questions: "What do we want
employees to do differently to support the business?"
and "Why aren't they already doing it?" The answers to
the second question will yield the greatest insights. Is it
that they don't have the knowledge or skills? Or is it that
they don't have sufficient tools or infrastructure? Is it a
question of motivation? And if it's a question of motivation, do people need to be spurred to work harder or
smarter? Many of Hiram's metrics were based on the
assumption that the organization wasn't working hard
enough, but that's usually not the case in most companies. Overwhelmingly, I think, people want to do a good
job. Has anyone asked the warehouse workers why some
orders weren't being delivered on time?

There is no evidence that Hiram sought any input from employees on the design of his measures, and I suspect that his approach to rolling out the new program featured information versus communication and education. If he wanted buy-in from employees, he should have gone much further than simply telling them what their goals were, helping them instead to genuinely understand why those objectives mattered to the business and to shareholders. He should have launched his program as a pilot and made it clear to employees that it would be refined based on their experience and input.

Even better, at the outset, he could have explained the company's goals and then let employees own the process of defining how the goals should be reached and how progress toward them should be measured. I remember a time I was advising a client who ran a mine in Wyoming. Management wanted to bring down costs and had placed incentives for savings on all the factors that influenced costs. The company found itself paying out bonuses, yet the profitability of the mine didn't improve. We were asked to investigate, and since the quantitative results were inconclusive, we went to Wyoming for some qualitative feedback. We asked the workers, "Is there anything you've done in the past 12 months that you might not have done if not for the bonus plan?" There was: They had shut off some of the faucets to conserve water. The problem was, less water flow meant less throughput of the material they were extracting. So, yes, water conservation yielded a 12% improvement on that metric. But the ultimate outcome was that the operation made less money due to lower productivity.

This is a perfect example of how you become what you reward. By rewarding the wrong short-term performance, this company was missing the greater opportunity for long-term success.

VICE ADMIRAL DIEGO E. HERNÁNDEZ (U.S. NAVY, RETIRED) *is a management consultant in both the public and private sectors and serves on a number of corporate boards. He is based in Miami Lakes, Florida.*

Let's spend a moment assessing Hiram's job performance over the past year. In that short period of time, he has managed to create a climate of uncertainty and self-preservation among employees by reducing the workforce in two poorly planned increments. He has eliminated workers without reducing the amount of work. He has established the wrong metrics for customer service, shipping, and R&D. He has arrested the development of the company's next generation of salespeople. He has delayed the launch of a breakthrough product. He has publicly humiliated company employees. And he has succeeded in teaching Rainbarrel's workers that the best use of their time and energy is in devising ways to game the system.

Is it any surprise that rank-and-file employees aren't sufficiently focused on what is good for the company? Their leaders obviously aren't.

Yes, I would say that Hiram needs to rethink his approach.

But I would hasten to add that Rainbarrel's problems don't begin and end with the CFO and his performance metrics. He is clearly oblivious to what his actions have done to the company, but he is not the only one. The CEO, first and foremost, doesn't seem to be paying attention to his people or his customers. The VP of human resources says he doesn't know what to make of the apparent decline in morale. The products division president knew he had a product breakthrough that was not funded but did not raise the issue with the CEO. The chief counsel knew that many of the patents he was reviewing were not commercially viable. There is something fundamentally wrong in a company where executives do not communicate openly and continually with one another about the business—where they do not question questionable things. Is it any surprise that rank-and-file employees aren't sufficiently focused on what is good for the company? Their leaders obviously aren't.

Effective performance management begins with clear two-way communications to ensure goals are understood and accepted. Even more, it requires multiple feedback channels for employees so that they can inform managers of any problem areas in their jobs. Senior managers cannot make good decisions without knowing the truth, and at Rainbarrel, they aren't hearing it.

When it comes to improving individual performance, I would urge Rainbarrel's management to look beyond pay for performance and make more effective use of intangible rewards. Public recognition, a letter of appreciation, or a word of praise can do a great deal to focus an individual's attention on organizational targets. Such motivational tools are powerful yet terribly underused in business settings.

That bias comes from my naval experience, no doubt. Leaders in the U.S. armed services have no control over compensation levels and don't have the option of giving bonuses to high performers. We're intensely focused on mission achievement and realize that's entirely dependent on everyone buying in and giving it everything they've got—but the pay scales are set by Congress. How do we motivate people? We set high goals and communicate them simply and repeatedly. We take pains to establish valid metrics. We provide the means for people to achieve those goals, and we help remove the obstacles that always arise. In order to do that, we listen to people's concerns and make use of multiple feedback loops so we can hear the truth. We create interim goals and publicly recognize interim successes. We differentiate, with an aim to promoting the top performers and getting rid of underperformers. And we do all this continuously. In the end, our people identify strongly with the goals of the organization and feel energized when they achieve these goals. And I can testify that there is nothing more electrifying to a leader than obtaining that level of commitment.

Right now, Rainbarrel's management is witnessing the opposite condition. Employees are thoroughly alienated, for good reason, and they will have to reconnect with the company before anything good can happen. Management's immediate focus should be to create the conditions that will allow employees to achieve Rainbarrel's goals and to find ways to acknowledge and reward those achievements. Metrics are important, but the key to high performance is within people.

BARRY LESKIN *was the chief learning officer for ChevronTexaco, the human resources partner at Ernst & Young, UK, and the chairman of the management and organization department at the University of Southern California's Marshall School of Business. He is now an independent consultant.*

Unfortunately for Rainbarrel, it needs to spend some time undoing the damage done by Hiram Phillips. As soon as possible, the CEO should focus on two change strategies for short-term and systemwide performance improvement: selecting performance-driven leaders and aligning the performance culture with the company's strategic direction.

Research has demonstrated that a company's top performers in mid- to senior-level jobs have a tremendous effect on corporate outcomes—that is, these top performers are 50% more productive than their average-performing counterparts. That means it's imperative to identify and develop these significant contributors early on, ensure that they have the right skills, and then place them in high-level positions.

A company achieves its greatest advantage when performance culture and strategy reinforce each other.

Doing so may be one of the most effective ways to build and sustain a strong performance culture and, in turn, improve performance.

That said, creating a strong performance culture isn't enough to change overall performance. A company must also align its performance and reward culture with its strategies. Indeed, a well-communicated strategy, with an integrated set of activities to support it, can itself signal to employees what senior executives really value, even if the leaders are advocating one set of behaviors and unintentionally rewarding another. But a company achieves its greatest advantage when performance culture and strategy reinforce each other and senior leaders consistently reward the activities they advocate.

Selecting the right leaders and aligning culture with strategy, though critical to performance, are considered by some to be "soft" initiatives, and their importance may be underestimated by leaders who focus mainly on results. Such leaders are apt to continually seek engineering solutions to people issues—to no avail.

Hiram seems to fit this description. He has introduced performance metrics without thinking them through or consulting other business-unit heads about how these changes will affect the company. He has actually hurt performance. And Keith Randall isn't any better. After all, he chose Hiram as a leader. What does this tell you about his understanding of how to lead organizational change? What signal has he sent to employees about his criteria for selecting senior leaders, and how does this affect his credibility?

During my career as a consultant and HR executive, I've seen many companies like Rainbarrel that unintentionally discourage employee behaviors that might increase corporate performance. For instance, top executives at one company tried to measure individuals' performance and leadership skills by asking in a 360-degree survey "to what extent the leader provides consequences to those who commit to performance contracts and miss them." The problem was, high scores on this item, meaning the leader was likely to provide consequences, had a low correlation with "effective leadership" in the survey. In other words, those who provided consequences were less likely to be seen as competent leaders by subordinates and peers. So in effect, the company was signaling that it valued relationships and harmony over results.

Many companies also discourage behaviors like challenging the status quo and raising difficult issues, which are essential to corporate performance. When candidates who display these behaviors are up for high-level positions, they often lose out because they're considered rebellious or in need of "polish."

Just as illogical is the way that pay-for-performance plays out in most companies. The whole point of such schemes is to differentiate and improve individual performance. But since employees know their target bonus, and the bonus pools are zero-sum, it's impossible for a manager to give one individual an outsize reward without penalizing one or more average performers, however slightly. Faced with this outcome, managers routinely default to the same target for everyone, fearful of demotivating the average performers. And that reluctance undermines all the power of performance-based pay, effectively punishing the high performers.

I could offer up more in this vein, but my point is simple. If Keith Randall selects the right leaders, communicates a clear set of goals, and aligns the company's performance culture with its strategy, results will be achieved—slowly in the short term, perhaps, but exponentially faster over time.

Originally published in January 2003
Reprint R0301A

Moving Mountains

BRONWYN FRYER

Executive Summary

WHAT COULD BE MORE fundamental to management,
or more difficult, than motivating people? After all, a
manager, by definition, is someone who gets work done
through others. But how? A typical recipe for motivation
calls for a mixture of persuasion, encouragement, and
compulsion. Yet the best leaders, we suspect, need no
recipe: They get people to produce great results by
appealing to their deepest drives, needs, and desires.
And so we discovered when we asked a dozen of the
world's top leaders to describe how they each met a
daunting challenge in motivating an individual, a team,
or an organization.

Their answers are as varied as human nature. Some of
the leaders appeal to people's need for the rational and
the orderly: Mattel's Robert Eckert emphasized the reassuring power of delivering a consistent message, and

HP's Carly Fiorina focuses on facing hard truths and setting step-by-step goals. Some, like celebrated oceanographer Robert Ballard, Pfizer CEO Hank McKinnell, and BP America president Ross Pillari, see the powerful motivating effects of asking people to rise to difficult challenges. Others focus more on the human spirit, appealing to the desire to do something, as BMW's Chris Bangle puts it, "rare, marvelous, and lasting."

And quite a few inspire though example, as Dial chairman Herb Baum did when he donated $1,000 from his bonus to each of the company's 155 lowest-paid people. "If you draw the line on your greed, and your employees see it," he says, "they will be incredibly loyal and perform much better for you." And he has the numbers to prove it. "Right now," he adds, "we're experiencing our lowest level of attrition in 11 years, and we're tracking toward another banner year because people are happy."

THERE'S NO TRICK TO motivating others. It requires a clear, unbiased understanding of the situation at hand, deep insight into the vagaries of human nature at both the individual and the group levels, the establishment of appropriate and reasonable expectations and goals, and the construction of a balanced set of tangible and intangible incentives. It requires, in other words, hard thinking and hard work. And when an organization is under strain or is in crisis, the challenges—and the stakes—become that much higher.

The questions that managers have to grapple with as they try to inspire their people are many and complex: How do you deal with individuals or groups at different

motivation levels that vary in different ways? How can
you influence the behavior of a single individual, let
alone an organization of hundreds or thousands? How
can you help people feel enthusiastic and committed,
especially in difficult times? To find out how such questions have been answered in practice, we asked nine
business leaders—along with a high school teacher, an
undersea explorer, and a champion sled dog racer—to
describe how they met a daunting challenge in motivating an individual, a team, or an organization. Here's what
they had to say.

Start with the Truth

*Carly Fiorina is chairman and CEO of Hewlett-Packard
in Palo Alto, California.*

My biggest motivation challenge has been to reinvent
HP in a way that celebrates its great history as a company while moving it forward. Doing that has required
me to help people first to confront reality, then to set
high aspirations, and finally to march pragmatically from
reality to aspiration.

Honest confrontation is tough. I remember my
first meeting with 700 of our senior leaders, when we
underwent this very realistic self-appraisal about our
customers, our competitive
situation, and our performance. You can't do your
own interpretation of what's
wrong and beat people up; to
motivate them to change,
you have to show them a
mirror. So on the white board, I wrote down comments
these managers had themselves made two years earlier

*The process of doing
begets progress; along the
way, you must remind
people of how far they've
come already.*

about the company, including the comment that HP was too slow and indecisive. I also wrote down things customers had said about us, both good and bad. When confronted with the inescapable facts of what they had said about themselves and what customers had told us, managers accepted the truth.

Once you have the truth, people need aspirational goals. To cross that uncomfortable gap between the truth and the goal, you must set very achievable, step-by-step measures. The process of doing begets progress; along the way, you must remind people of how far they've come already and how much closer they are to achieving the goal. That's when you see the light in their eyes. All these things—honest self-assessment, setting goals, and marching toward them—form a constant process, and they are also what make managing fun.

Appeal to Greatness

Christopher Bangle is global chief of design at BMW in Munich, Germany.

Recently, my design group met a huge challenge—one that ended up inspiring the whole company. The new modern-art museum here in Munich—the *Pinakothek der Moderne,* which opened in September—invited BMW to put something on permanent display in time for the opening. Of course, doing any kind of installation demands a lot of time, and we didn't even hear about the offer until June. So I nixed the idea—we were too busy designing cars.

Our communications director begged me to reconsider, so I went to look at the museum space. Suddenly, I got excited by the idea of doing something truly grand. But to do it, I had to sell our board on the crazy idea of doing an enormously expensive, distracting design project that would bring in no revenue.

My argument went something like this: "Gentlemen, this is a once-in-a-lifetime cultural opportunity with the newest, largest design museum in Europe." Fortunately, art is a great motivator; the desire to contribute to something lasting is enormous. They approved, and we went to work. And work we did, with the kind of intensity and passion that comes with the knowledge that one is achieving something rare and marvelous.

Eighty days after first hearing of the project, 50 days after the board approved it, and 40 days after concept freeze, the museum opened with our gigantic installation, "The Art of Car Design." It's a lavishly shaped work occupying a 10×14 meter wall, consisting of 50 tons of milled Carrara marble, six screens displaying video loops, dynamic lighting, and more. On seeing it for the first time, one of the board members said to me, "Herr Bangle, you can be proud of this." And I replied, "No, you can be proud of this. You are a Medici."

Make Them Proud

*2002 National Teacher of the Year, **Chauncey Veatch** works at Coachella Valley High School in Thermal, California.*

My student "José" serves as a reminder of the power of motivation—which, for me, is about respecting my students and providing a way for them to contribute. Like so many of our students, José comes from a rural, migrant Hispanic family of modest means. He entered my American History class in the second semester of his junior year as a special-education student. He had difficulty writing in English or Spanish and a history of frequent altercations at school. If he heard the word "fight," he deemed it an engraved invitation to participate, a social event not to be missed.

The first step in motivating José was to celebrate the gifts he brought to class. Though he had trouble writing, he could speak cogently about concepts; our goal was to help him get his thoughts on paper. He loved music, and the poetry of rapper Tupac Shakur intrigued him, so we tied his interest in rap music into our studies of the American Civil Rights movement. At every mention of the lyrics of contemporary music in the lesson, his ears perked up.

José was given every opportunity to shine before his peers. In an exam one day, I asked students to explain one branch of government as laid out in the Constitution. He raised his hand and asked, "What's the name of that French dude who wrote about the separation of powers?" This was not a throwaway moment. So I asked him to explain, and he responded, "You know, the idea that the Congress, judges, and the president shouldn't be more powerful than each other because if one branch gets too strong it can become a dictator?" I stopped the exam right there and said to the class, "José, the answer to your question is Montesquieu—and you've just shown you really understand a key point that I wish more Americans understood." My entire class stood up and applauded him. They knew what he had overcome.

Stick to Your Values

L.M. Baker, Jr., is chairman of Wachovia in Charlotte, North Carolina.

Most people think motivating people is about pushing others to do what you want them to do, but I've found that the secret to motivating others has really been to adhere to simple values, things like honesty, fairness, and generosity.

One of my biggest challenges was motivating myself to go into business in the first place. I started out in life thinking I was going to be a poet. I studied English in college but then found myself in Vietnam. By the time I got out of the Marine Corps, the only things I knew how to do were write poetry and conduct night combat patrols.

I've never been asked to compromise my own standards or values; that's how I stay motivated, and that's how I strive to motivate others.

So I decided that to make a living I'd have to go to business school. At the time—this was 35 years ago—my wife and I disapproved of what we saw as the power and greed that often attend big business. When I took my first job as a management trainee, we agreed that I could give this business thing a try, but if either of us felt that business was compromising our values, we'd leave it behind. So I went to work in a commercial bank. All these years later, I'm delighted to say I was never once asked to compromise my own standards or values. That's how I stay motivated, and that's how I strive to motivate others.

Be a Broken Record

Robert A. Eckert is chairman and CEO of Mattel in El Segundo, California.

People can't and won't do much for you if no one in the organization knows what's going on, what you expect of them, and what the future holds. And talking to them once a quarter isn't enough—you have to repeat messages of direction, inspiration, and comfort daily, in a variety of forms.

When I first got to Mattel, the company was in transition. In addition to spending major face time with all the senior managers, I spent hours and hours describing to all our employees and other stakeholders where we were going and how we were going to get there. I traveled and met with people, of course, but I also set up a program of regular e-mail updates, invited two-way communication, and responded personally to employee messages. Today, the company is back on track, but I'm still constantly communicating—in the elevator, in the cafeteria, on the street, on the phone, on planes, and through e-mails. And it's always the same basic message, which is our vision for the company.

People can't and won't do much for you if no one in the organization knows what's going on.

I've found that this constant and consistent communication, while at times sounding like a broken record, is the single most reassuring thing I can do for all stakeholders: employees, investors, customers, media, and senior management. When employees hear what's going on from me first, they feel part of the team and most of all, respected, and that motivates them to come to work every day.

Build Trust

Susan Butcher is a four-time winner of the 1,150-mile Iditarod sled dog race.

When I talk about motivation, I'm not talking about people; I'm talking about motivating my sled dog team and each dog individually. Dogs are very intelligent, and you can't make them do anything they don't want to do. If they don't trust you, they won't go along with you.

My experience during the 1983 Iditarod is a good example. Back then, the trail was poorly marked, and I was a young musher. At one point, we got completely lost; I must have turned the team around 25 times over many hours looking for the trail. The dogs finally lost confidence in me. They'll forgive a few mistakes, but if you send them in the wrong direction too many times, they'll just stop. And that's what happened. With a lot of effort, I eventually convinced them to get moving. At times I had to walk in front of them for as much as 20 miles at a time. We finished in ninth place, after slipping below 20th. After we pulled into Nome, every single experienced musher told me that I'd never be able to use that team again, that the dogs would never recover their confidence. They thought the dogs had lost faith in themselves, but I knew they had lost faith in me.

So I set out to regain their trust. I taught them what "I'm sorry" means, so they'd know it was not their fault if I made mistakes. I simplified my commands so I could communicate with them even more clearly than I had before. And I put us into extremely challenging situations, so they learned that together we could always get out of trouble. At the same time, I let them know that I trusted them—that they could take the lead in the wilderness and challenge my commands if I put us in danger. For example, they're better than I am at spotting thin ice.

Over the course of the year, every dog regained full confidence in me and in the team. That same team took me to a very close second place the next year, and we went on to victory in 1986.

Encourage Risk

Ross J. Pillari is the president of BP America in Warrenville, Illinois, and is a group vice president of London-based BP PLC.

Helping people to try things that feel personally risky is the toughest motivational challenge. I experienced this firsthand when my own tolerance for risk was tested in the early 1990s.

I was running BP's U.S. retail operation. At that time, Lord Browne, BP's chief executive, asked me to be global chief of staff for BP's research and engineering operation and help it become more commercial. Browne thought I was the right person to come in and help the group think more like a business. I thought the new role was a terrible idea.

I was a marketer, not a scientist; I couldn't speak the language of science, and I certainly didn't have what I thought was the skill set necessary to lead a group of mathematicians and geologists. Why would I want to risk my career by accepting a job where success seemed so unlikely?

Browne didn't try to talk me into it. But he did get me to talk openly about where I saw risks to myself and to the organization. He also made it clear that I wasn't assuming all the risk on my own. I accepted the job, and we were successful in turning the R&D group into a more commercially focused enterprise. Personally, it was probably the most broadening assignment of my career.

What I learned from this experience and what guides my thinking about motivation today is that you can't, and you don't want to, eliminate all risks. But you can help a person step into that slightly uncomfortable space where people and organizations achieve extraordinary results.

The best way is through open and frank discussion about the likelihood of success, by making roles and account-abilities crystal clear, by spreading the risk across the team and the organization, and by providing visible and confident support regardless of the end result.

Care for the Little Guy

Herb Baum is chairman, president, and CEO of the Dial Corporation in Scottsdale, Arizona.

People at the top of their organizations—the people who make the most money—often forget how hard it is for the people at the bottom. If the leader can make the people at the bottom feel like they're cared for, the entire organization will feel inspired and motivated.

My first CEO job was at Quaker State Corporation, which was headquartered in the little town of Oil City, Pennsylvania. The people who lived in this town and worked for the company lived modestly, and every dollar they earned mattered to them. I remember sitting with some of these folks and hearing how they went about buying even the most basic things, like shoes for their kids. After I heard that, I gave back the company car.

If you draw the line on your own greed, and your employees see it, they will be incredibly loyal and perform much better for you.

Today, the people at the bottom of my company are raising families on earnings of somewhere between $25,000 and $45,000 a year. Last year, they would have earned a bonus of about $500, while people at the top were making bonuses many times that size. So I went to the board and asked permission to give each of the 155 people who make the lowest salaries $1,000 from my own bonus. To me and most CEOs, $1,000 is a drop in the bucket. But for people trying to put a child through school or covering the health costs of a sick parent, it's a lot of money, and it helps.

If you draw the line on your own greed, and your employees see it, they will be incredibly loyal and perform much better for you. Right now, we're experiencing our lowest level of attrition in 11 years, and we're tracking toward another banner year because people are happy.

Ground Without Grinding

Mario Mazzola is the chief development officer at Cisco Systems in San Jose, California.

One of the hardest things about motivating others is creating a challenge that stimulates the energy and interest of bright people while keeping them anchored. If people are already reaching for the sky, you need to gently ground them without discouraging them.

On a personal level, I try to do this with my 13-year-old daughter. She has a penchant for mathematics and frequently will work ahead, something generally to be encouraged. But then she'll solve problems with more complex formulas than necessary. To encourage her to master the basics and learn the

If people are already reaching for the sky, you need to ground them without discouraging them.

importance of simpler solutions, I will set her little problems that require her to include basic mathematical concepts, like derivatives. The idea is to give her a little challenge that also requires discipline, imagination, and self-confidence.

At work, I have another scenario. I manage a group of highly motivated, smart engineers who typically come up with the most efficient, innovative way to develop new technologies. The problem is that our customers work with existing technologies that require integration, which creates a much more complex problem. To keep the engineers from feeling frustrated at having to craft a more complex solution, I first genuinely acknowledge their ingenuity. Second, I have them meet with customers, so they can really understand and appreciate the customers' situations. That motivates them to drive through the homestretch and create technologies that are both innovative and meet current needs.

Leap First, Ask Later

Robert D. Ballard, whose team discovered the Titanic, *the* Bismarck, *and* PT-109, *is the president of the Institute for Exploration in Mystic, Connecticut, and director of the University of Rhode Island's Institute for Underwater Archaeology at its Graduate School of Oceanography.*

Some people think motivating people means coaxing, wheedling, and persuading them to adopt your point of view. But when the stakes are high or you're in an emergency, persuasion is out of the question. You just have to make the deal first, then figure out how to get there. When they realize there's no other way out, the team just gets the job done—and brilliantly.

We ran into a situation like this not long ago, when my team was preparing to film an underwater exploration at the Galápagos Islands for the Jason Project, which allows schoolchildren to view live dives from their classrooms. We had gathered $6 million in expensive telecommunication equipment, and the government of

Ecuador offered to have its navy tow all of it to the islands for us. We accepted the offer, and then a week before we were to film, the barge sank 600 miles offshore.

A quarter-million schoolchildren had studied the Galápagos all year in preparation for this dive; to me, canceling the broadcast was totally out of the question. So we organized the biggest equipment scavenger hunt in existence. We divided 20 people into teams and got on the phones, gathering loans and donations from every possible source—universities, organizations, governments, individuals. I remember the CIA loaned us a plane. The team had all this stuff delivered to a warehouse in Miami, then flown to California and from there to Ecuador.

A week after the barge sank, we went live, on schedule, and all those school kids never knew the difference. As a result of this experience, the team knew it could do just about anything—and in very short order.

Set Different Incentive Levels

Liu Chuanzhi is chairman of Legend Group of Beijing.

Our challenge has been to motivate three distinctly different groups—executive team members, middle managers, and the rest of our line employees. We have different expectations for each group, and they each require different kinds of incentives.

Our executive team needs a sense of ownership in the company. Many state-owned enterprises in China face a special challenge: They cannot give their senior executives stock. But we took an untraditional approach; we reformed our ownership structure to make Legend a joint stock company, enabling us to give all our executive team members stock. In addition, senior executives need recognition, so we provide them with opportunities to speak to the media. To date, we've lost no senior executives to other companies.

Midlevel managers want to become senior managers, so they respond best to challenges—to opportunities to display and hone their talents. We set very high performance standards for our middle managers, and we let them participate in strategic processes, in designing their own work, and in making and executing their own decisions. If they get good results, they are handsomely rewarded.

Line employees need a sense of stability. If they take responsibility and are conscientious, they earn a predictable bonus. We also tie team performance to company or unit performance, and individual performance to team performance. For example, we might let the team decide how to allocate a percentage of their team bonus to individuals, with some general guidelines from the corporate level.

Work Quickly Through Pain

Hank McKinnell is the chairman and CEO of Pfizer in New York.

You motivate people by moving quickly toward a goal, especially if getting to the goal involves pain. Knowing that the organization is committed to quick, decisive action frees people to think creatively and work in concert.

We saw this in the integration of Pfizer and Warner-Lambert in 2000. We won our bid for the company, but what we won was a firm thoroughly demoralized by a takeover battle. In my first meetings with the transition teams, I emphasized that we had to build a new company quickly, particularly before our largest competitor settled its own merger issues. The vision was ambitious—integrate Pfizer and Warner-Lambert, seek best practices where appropriate, and be ready to operate as a totally unified organization barely five months after the two companies agreed to the union.

The emphasis on speed tamps down resentment, turf issues, and "paralysis by analysis."

Time was not our friend; our traditional approach of consensus building wasn't going to work. So we gave people permission to move fast and to make mistakes— as long as their actions were in keeping with our values of integrity, performance, and respect for people. The emphasis on speed tamped down resentment, turf issues, and "paralysis by analysis." In our U.S. sales force alone, for example, teams from both companies recommended more than 200 changes in operations and policies, and nearly all of them were accepted. Ultimately, hundreds of transition teams, composed of excellent people from both companies, knit together a nearly seamless new Pfizer that was totally operational just a few hours after signing the closing papers.

Originally published in January 2003
Reprint R0301B

Pygmalion in Management

J. STERLING LIVINGSTON

Executive Summary

WHAT HAS LONG BEEN RECOGNIZED by teachers, physicians, and behavioral scientists holds true for management: One person's expectations shape another person's behavior. If a manger has high expectations, employees are likely to excel; if expectations are low, employees will likely respond with poor performance.

In this HBR classic article from 1969, Livingston draws on numerous case studies and other research to demonstrate the importance of managerial expectations to individual and group performance. Consider the insurance executive who identified his six best agents and assigned them to his most capable manager. Not surprisingly, this group surpassed its already ambitious target. Equally unsurprising was what happened to a group of low producers assigned to the company's least capable manager. Their performance declined even further. But what

173

happened to the group of average agents assigned to an average manager? That group increased its productivity by a higher percentage than the top group, because the manager refused to consider herself—or her agents—less capable than the superstars.

If managers believe that employees will perform poorly, they can't hide their expectations. Indeed, when managers think they're concealing their low expectations, they show through the most. And their high expectations often do not come through clearly enough.

Manager's beliefs about themselves influence how they view and treat their employees. Superior managers have high expectations based primarily on what they think of their own abilities to select, train, and motivate people. They give up on employees reluctantly, because that means giving up on themselves.

Most parents are aware that teachers' expectations about individual children become self-fulfilling prophecies: If a teacher believes a child is slow, the child will come to believe that, too, and will indeed learn slowly. The lucky child who strikes a teacher as bright also picks up on that expectation and will rise to fulfill it. This finding has been confirmed so many times, and in such varied settings, that it's no longer even debated.

Self-fulfilling prophecies, it turns out, are just as prevalent in offices as they are in elementary school classrooms. If a manager is convinced that the people in her group are first-rate, they'll reliably outperform a group whose manager believes the reverse—even if the innate talent of the two groups is similar.

J. Sterling Livingston named this 1969 article after the mythical sculptor who carves a statue of a woman that is brought to life. His title also pays homage to George Bernard Shaw, whose play Pygmalion *explores the notion that the way one person treats another can, for better or worse, be transforming. In his article, Livingston notes that creating positive expectations is remarkably difficult, and he offers guidelines for managers: Focus special attention on an employee's first year because that's when expectations are set, make sure new hires get matched with outstanding supervisors, and set high expectations for yourself.*

IN GEORGE BERNARD SHAW'S *Pygmalion*, Eliza Doolittle explains: "You see, really and truly, apart from the things anyone can pick up (the dressing and the proper way of speaking, and so on), the difference between a lady and a flower girl is not how she behaves but how she's treated. I shall always be a flower girl to Professor Higgins because he always treats me as a flower girl and always will; but I know I can be a lady to you because you always treat me as a lady and always will."

Some managers always treat their subordinates in a way that leads to superior performance. But most managers, like Professor Higgins, unintentionally treat their subordinates in a way that leads to lower performance than they are capable of achieving. The way managers treat their subordinates is subtly influenced by what they expect of them. If managers' expectations are high, productivity is likely to be excellent. If their expectations are low, productivity is likely to be poor. It is as though there were a law that caused subordinates' performance to rise or fall to meet managers' expectations.

The powerful influence of one person's expectations on another's behavior has long been recognized by physicians and behavioral scientists and, more recently, by teachers. But heretofore the importance of managerial expectations for individual and group performance has not been widely understood. I have documented this phenomenon in a number of case studies prepared during the past decade for major industrial concerns. These cases and other evidence available from scientific research now reveal:

- What managers expect of subordinates and the way they treat them largely determine their performance and career progress.

- A unique characteristic of superior managers is the ability to create high performance expectations that subordinates fulfill.

- Less effective managers fail to develop similar expectations, and as a consequence, the productivity of their subordinates suffers.

- Subordinates, more often than not, appear to do what they believe they are expected to do.

Impact on Productivity

One of the most comprehensive illustrations of the effect of managerial expectations on productivity is recorded in studies of the organizational experiment undertaken in 1961 by Alfred Oberlander, manager of the Rockaway district office of the Metropolitan Life Insurance Company. He had observed that outstanding insurance agen-

cies grew faster than average or poor agencies and that
new insurance agents performed better in outstanding
agencies than in average or poor agencies, regardless of
their sales aptitude. He decided, therefore, to group his
superior agents in one unit to stimulate their performance and to provide a challenging environment in
which to introduce new salespeople.

Accordingly, Oberlander assigned his six best agents
to work with his best assistant manager, an equal number of average producers to work with an average assistant manager, and the remaining low producers to work
with the least able manager. He then asked the superior
group to produce two-thirds of the premium volume
achieved by the entire agency during the previous year.
He describes the results as follows:

"Shortly after this selection had been made, the people in the agency began referring to this select group as
a 'superstaff' because of their high esprit de corps in
operating so well as a unit. Their production efforts
over the first 12 weeks far surpassed our most opti-
mistic expectations . . . proving that groups of people
of sound ability can be motivated beyond their apparently normal productive capacities when the problems
created by the poor producers are eliminated from the
operation.

"Thanks to this fine result, our overall agency performance improved by 40%, and it remained at this figure.

"In the beginning of 1962 when, through expansion,
we appointed another assistant manager and assigned
him a staff, we again used this same concept, arranging
the agents once more according to their productive
capacity.

"The assistant managers were assigned . . . according
to their ability, with the most capable assistant manager

receiving the best group, thus playing strength to
strength. Our agency overall production again improved
by about 25% to 30%, and so this staff arrangement
remained in place until the end of the year.

"Now in this year of 1963, we found upon analysis that
there were so many agents . . . with a potential of half a
million dollars or more that only one staff remained of
those people in the agency who were not considered to
have any chance of reaching the half-million-dollar
mark."

Although the productivity of the superstaff improved
dramatically, it should be pointed out that the productivity of those in the lowest unit, "who were not considered
to have any chance of reaching the half-million-dollar
mark," actually declined, and that attrition among them
increased. The performance of the superior agents rose
to meet their managers' expectations, while that of the
weaker ones declined as predicted.

SELF-FULFILLING PROPHECIES

The "average" unit, however, proved to be an anomaly.
Although the district manager expected only average
performance from this group, its productivity increased
significantly. This was because the assistant manager in
charge of the group refused to believe that she was less
capable than the manager of the superstaff or that the
agents in the top group had any greater ability than the
agents in her group. She insisted in discussions with her
agents that every person in the middle group had greater
potential than those in the superstaff, lacking only their
years of experience in selling insurance. She stimulated
her agents to accept the challenge of outperforming the
superstaff. As a result, each year the middle group

increased its productivity by a higher percentage than
the superstaff did (although it did not attain the dollar
volume of the top group).

It is of special interest that the self-image of the manager of the average unit did not permit her to accept others' treatment of her as an average manager, just as Eliza
Doolittle's image of herself as a lady did not permit her
to accept others' treatment of her as a flower girl. The
assistant manager transmitted her own feelings of efficacy to her agents, created mutual expectancy of high
performance, and greatly stimulated productivity. Com-
parable results occurred when a similar experiment was
made at another office of the company.

Further confirmation comes from a study of the early
managerial experiences of 49 college graduates who were
management-level employees of an operating company
of AT&T. David E. Berlew and Douglas T. Hall of the
Massachusetts Institute of Technology examined the
career progress of these managers over a period of five
years and discovered that their relative success, as measured by salary increases and the company's estimate of
each one's performance and potential, depended largely
on the company's expectations.

The influence of one person's expectations on
another's behavior is by no means a business discovery.
More than half a century ago, Albert Moll concluded
from his clinical experience that subjects behaved as
they believed they were expected to. The phenomenon he
observed, in which "the prophecy causes its own fulfill-
ment," has recently become a subject of considerable scientific interest. For example:

- In a series of scientific experiments, Robert Rosenthal
  of Harvard University has demonstrated that a

"teacher's expectation for a pupil's intellectual competence can come to serve as an educational self-fulfilling prophecy."

- An experiment in a summer Headstart program for 60
  preschoolers compared the performance of pupils
  under (a) teachers who had been led to expect relatively slow learning by their children, and (b) teachers
  who had been led to believe that their children had
  excellent intellectual ability and learning capacity.
  Pupils of the second group of teachers learned much
  faster.[1]

Moreover, the healing professions have long recognized that a physician's or psychiatrist's expectations
can have a formidable influence on a patient's physical
or mental health. What takes place in the minds of the
patients and the healers, particularly when they have
congruent expectations, may determine the outcome.
For instance, the havoc of a doctor's pessimistic progno-
sis has often been observed. Again, it is well known that
the efficacy of a new drug or a new treatment can be
greatly influenced by the physician's expectations—a
result referred to by the medical profession as a placebo
effect.

PATTERN OF FAILURE

When salespersons are treated by their managers as
superpeople, as the superstaff was at the Metropolitan
Rockaway district office, they try to live up to that image
and do what they know supersalespersons are expected
to do. But when the agents with poor productivity
records are treated by their managers as *not* having any
chance of success, as the low producers at Rockaway

were, this negative expectation also becomes a managerial self-fulfilling prophecy.

Unsuccessful salespersons have great difficulty maintaining their self-image and self-esteem. In response to low managerial expectations, they typically attempt to prevent additional damage to their egos by avoiding situations that might lead to greater failure. They either reduce the number of sales calls they make or avoid trying to close sales when that might result in further painful rejection, or both. Low expectations and damaged egos lead them to behave in a manner that increases the probability of failure, thereby fulfilling their managers' expectations. Let me illustrate:

Not long ago I studied the effectiveness of branch bank managers at a West Coast bank with over 500 branches. The managers who had had their lending authority reduced because of high rates of loss became progressively less effective. To prevent further loss of authority, they turned to making only "safe" loans. This action resulted in losses of business to competing banks and a relative decline in both deposits and profits at their branches. Then, to reverse that decline in deposits and earnings, they often "reached" for loans and became almost irrational in their acceptance of questionable credit risks. Their actions were not so much a matter of poor judgment as an expression of their willingness to take desperate risks in the hope of being able to avoid further damage to their egos and to their careers.

Thus, in response to the low expectations of their supervisors who had reduced their lending authority, they behaved in a manner that led to larger credit losses. They appeared to do what they believed they were expected to do, and their supervisors' expectations became self-fulfilling prophecies.

Power of Expectations

Managers cannot avoid the depressing cycle of events that flow from low expectations merely by hiding their feelings from subordinates. If managers believe subordinates will perform poorly, it is virtually impossible for them to mask their expectations because the message usually is communicated unintentionally, without conscious action on their part.

Indeed, managers often communicate most when they believe they are communicating least. For instance, when they say nothing—become cold and uncommunicative—it usually is a sign that they are displeased by a subordinate or believe that he or she is hopeless. The silent treatment communicates negative feelings even more effectively, at times, than a tongue-lashing does. What seems to be critical in the communication of expectations is not what the boss says so much as the way he or she behaves. Indifferent and noncommittal treatment, more often than not, is the kind of treatment that communicates low expectations and leads to poor performance.

COMMON ILLUSIONS

Managers are more effective in communicating low expectations to their subordinates than in communicating high expectations to them, even though most managers believe exactly the opposite. It usually is astonishingly difficult for them to recognize the clarity with which they transmit negative feelings. To illustrate again:

- The Rockaway district manager vigorously denied that he had communicated low expectations to the agents in the poorest group who, he believed, did not have any chance of becoming high producers. Yet the message was clearly received by those agents. A typical case was that of an agent who resigned from the low unit. When the district manager told the agent that he was sorry she was leaving, the agent replied, "No you're not; you're glad." Although the district manager previously had said nothing to her, he had unintentionally communicated his low expectations to his agents through his indifferent manner. Subsequently, the agents who were assigned to the lowest unit interpreted the assignment as equivalent to a request for their resignation.

- One of the company's agency managers established superior, average, and low units, even though he was convinced that he had no superior or outstanding subordinates. "All my assistant managers and agents are either average or incompetent," he explained to the Rockaway district manager. Although he tried to duplicate the Rockaway results, his low opinions of his agents were communicated—not so subtly—to them. As a result, the experiment failed.

Positive feelings, on the other hand, often are not communicated clearly enough. Another insurance agency manager copied the organizational changes made at the Rockaway district office, grouping the salespeople she rated highly with the best manager, the average salespeople with an average manager, and so on. Improvement, however, did not result from the move. The Rockaway district manager therefore investigated the situation. He discovered that the assistant manager in charge of the high-performance unit was unaware that his manager considered him to be the best. In fact, he and the other agents doubted that the agency manager really believed there was any difference in their abilities.

This agency manager was a stolid, phlegmatic, unemotional woman who treated her agents in a rather pedestrian way. Since high expectations had not been communicated to them, they did not understand the reason for the new organization and could not see any point in it. Clearly, the way managers treat subordinates, not the way they organize them, is the key to high expectations and high productivity.

IMPOSSIBLE DREAMS

Managers' high expectations must pass the test of reality before they can be translated into performance. To become self-fulfilling prophecies, expectations must be made of sterner stuff than the power of positive thinking or generalized confidence in one's subordinates—helpful as these concepts may be for some other purposes. Subordinates will not be motivated to reach high levels of productivity unless they consider the boss's high expectations realistic and achievable. If they are encouraged to strive for unattainable goals, they eventually give up trying and settle for results that are lower than they are capable of achieving. The experience of a large electrical manufacturing company demonstrates this; the company discovered that production actually declined if production quotas were set too high, because the workers simply stopped trying to meet them. In other words, the practice of "dangling the carrot just beyond the donkey's reach," endorsed by many managers, is not a good motivational device.

Research by David C. McClelland of Harvard University and John W. Atkinson of the University of Michigan has demonstrated that the relationship of motivation to expectancy varies in the form of a bell-shaped curve.[2]

The degree of motivation and effort rises until the expectancy of success reaches 50%, then begins to fall even though the expectancy of success continues to increase. No motivation or response is aroused when the goal is perceived as being either virtually certain or virtually impossible to attain.

Moreover, as Berlew and Hall have pointed out, if subordinates fail to meet performance expectations that are close to their own level of aspirations, they will lower personal performance goals and standards, performance will tend to drop off, and negative attitudes will develop toward the activity or job.[3] It is therefore not surprising that failure of subordinates to meet the unrealistically high expectations of their managers leads to high rates of attrition, either voluntary or involuntary.

What managers believe about themselves subtly influences what they believe about their subordinates, what they expect of them, and how they treat them.

SECRET OF SUPERIORITY

Something takes place in the minds of superior managers that does not occur in the minds of those who are less effective. While superior managers are consistently able to create high performance expectations that their subordinates fulfill, weaker managers are not successful in obtaining a similar response. What accounts for the difference?

The answer, in part, seems to be that superior managers have greater confidence than other managers in their own ability to develop the talents of their subordinates. Contrary to what might be assumed, the high expectations of superior managers are based primarily on what they think about themselves—about their own ability to select, train, and motivate their subordinates. What managers believe about themselves subtly influences what they believe about their subordinates, what they expect of them, and how they treat them. If they have confidence in their ability to develop and stimulate subordinates to high levels of performance, they will expect much of them and will treat them with confidence that their expectations will be met. But if they have doubts about their ability to stimulate subordinates, they will expect less of them and will treat them with less confidence.

Stated in another way, the superior managers' record of success and confidence in their own ability give their high expectations credibility. As a consequence, their subordinates accept these expectations as realistic and try hard to achieve them.

The importance of what a manager believes about his or her training and motivational ability is illustrated by "Sweeney's Miracle," a managerial and educational self-fulfilling prophecy.

James Sweeney taught industrial management and psychiatry at Tulane University, and he also was responsible for the operation of the Biomedical Computer Center there. Sweeney believed that he could teach even a poorly educated man to be a capable computer operator. George Johnson, a former hospital porter, became janitor at the computer center; he was chosen by Sweeney to prove his conviction. In the mornings, Johnson performed his janitorial duties, and in the afternoons Sweeney taught him about computers.

Johnson was learning a great deal about computers when someone at the university concluded that to be a computer operator one had to have a certain IQ score.

Johnson was tested, and his IQ indicated that he would not be able to learn to type, much less operate a computer.

But Sweeney was not convinced. He threatened to quit unless Johnson was permitted to learn to program and operate the computer. Sweeney prevailed, and he is still running the computer center. Johnson is now in charge of the main computer room and is responsible for training new employees to program and operate the computer.[4]

Sweeney's expectations were based on what he believed about his own teaching ability, not on Johnson's learning credentials. What managers believe about their ability to train and motivate subordinates clearly is the foundation on which realistically high managerial expectations are built.

The Critical Early Years

Managerial expectations have their most magical influence on young people. As subordinates mature and gain experience, their self-image gradually hardens, and they begin to see themselves as their career records imply. Their own aspirations and the expectations of their superiors become increasingly controlled by the "reality" of their past performance. It becomes more and more difficult for them and for their managers to generate mutually high expectations unless they have outstanding records.

Incidentally, the same pattern occurs in school. Rosenthal's experiments with educational self-fulfilling prophecies consistently demonstrate that teachers' expectations are more effective in influencing intellectual growth in younger children than in older children. In the lower grade levels, particularly in the first and second grades, the effects of teachers' expectations are dramatic.

In the upper grade levels, teachers' prophecies seem to have little effect on children's intellectual growth, although they do affect their motivation and attitude toward school. While the declining influence of teachers' expectations cannot be completely explained, it is reasonable to conclude that younger children are more malleable, have fewer fixed notions about their abilities, and have less well established reputations in the schools. As they grow, particularly if they are assigned to "tracks" on the basis of their records, as is now often done in public schools, their beliefs about their intellectual ability and their teachers' expectations of them begin to harden and become more resistant to influence by others.

KEY TO FUTURE PERFORMANCE

The early years in a business organization, when young people can be strongly influenced by managerial expectations, are critical in determining future performance and career progress.

In their study at AT&T, Berlew and Hall concluded that the correlation between how much a company expects of an employee in the first year and how much that employee contributes during the next five years was "too compelling to be ignored."[5]

Subsequently, the two men studied the career records of 18 college graduates who were hired as management trainees in another of AT&T's operating companies. Again they found that both expectations and performance in the first year correlated consistently with later performance and success.

"Something important is happening in the first year. . . ," Berlew and Hall concluded. "Meeting high company expectations in the critical first year leads to the internalization of positive job attitudes and high standards; these attitudes and standards, in turn, would first lead to and be reinforced by strong performance and success in later years. It should

A young person's first manager is likely to be the most influential in that person's career.

also follow that a new manager who meets the challenge of one highly demanding job will be given subsequently a more demanding job, and his level of contribution will rise as he responds to the company's growing expectations of him. The key . . . is the concept of the first year as a *critical period for learning,* a time when the trainee is uniquely ready to develop or change in the direction of the company's expectations."[6]

MOST INFLUENTIAL BOSS

A young person's first manager is likely to be the most influential in that person's career. If managers are unable or unwilling to develop the skills young employees need to perform effectively, the latter will set lower personal standards than they are capable of achieving, their self-images will be impaired, and they will develop negative attitudes toward jobs, employers, and—in all probability—their own careers in business. Since the chances of building successful careers with these first employers will decline rapidly, the employees will leave, if they have high aspirations, in hope of finding better opportunities. If, on the other hand, early managers help employees achieve maximum potential, they will build the foundations for successful careers.

With few exceptions, the most effective branch managers at the West Coast bank were mature people in their forties and fifties. The bank's executives explained that it took considerable time for a person to gain the knowledge, experience, and judgment required to handle properly credit risks, customer relations, and employee relations.

One branch manager, however, ranked in the top 10% of the managers in terms of effectiveness (which included branch profit growth, deposit growth, scores on administrative audits, and subjective rankings by superiors), was only 27 years old. This young person had been made a branch manager at 25, and in two years had improved not only the performance of the branch substantially but also developed a younger assistant manager who, in turn, was made a branch manager at 25.

The assistant had had only average grades in college, but in just four years at the bank had been assigned to work with two branch managers who were remarkably effective teachers. The first boss, who was recognized throughout the bank for unusual skill in developing young people, did not believe that it took years to gain the knowledge and skill needed to become an effective banker. After two years, the young person was made assistant manager at a branch headed by another executive, who also was an effective developer of subordinates. Thus it was that the young person, when promoted to head a branch, confidently followed the model of two previous superiors in operating the branch, quickly established a record of outstanding performance, and trained an assistant to assume responsibility early.

For confirming evidence of the crucial role played by a person's first bosses, let us turn to selling, since performance in this area is more easily measured than in most managerial areas. Consider the following investigations:

- In a study of the careers of 100 insurance salespeople who began work with either highly competent or less-than-competent agency managers, the Life Insurance Agency Management Association found that those with average sales-aptitude test scores were nearly five times as likely to succeed under managers with good performance records as under managers with poor records, and those with superior sales-aptitude scores were found to be twice as likely to succeed under high-performing managers as they were under low-performing managers.[7]

- The Metropolitan Life Insurance Company determined in 1960 that differences in the productivity of new insurance agents who had equal sales aptitudes could be accounted for only by differences in the ability of managers in the offices to which they were assigned. Agents whose productivity was high in relation to their aptitude test scores invariably were employed in offices that had production records among the top third in the company. Conversely, those whose productivity was low in relation to their test scores typically were in the least successful offices. After analyzing all the factors that might have accounted for these variations, the company concluded that differences in the performance of new agents were due primarily to differences in the "proficiency in sales training and direction" of the local managers.[8]

- A study I conducted of the performance of automobile salespeople in Ford dealerships in New England revealed that superior salespersons were concentrated

in a few outstanding dealerships. For instance, ten of
the top 15 salespeople in New England were in three
(out of approximately 200) of the dealerships in this
region, and five of the top 15 people were in one highly
successful dealership. Yet four of these people previously had worked for other dealers without achieving
outstanding sales records. There was little doubt that
the training and motivational skills of managers in the
outstanding dealerships were critical.

ASTUTE SELECTION

While success in business sometimes appears to depend
on the luck of the draw, more than luck is involved when
a young person is selected by a superior manager. Successful managers do not pick their subordinates at ran-
dom or by the toss of a coin. They are careful to select
only those who they "know" will succeed. As Metropolitan's Rockaway district manager, Alfred Oberlander,
insisted: "Every man or woman who starts with us is
going to be a top-notch life insurance agent, or he or she
would not have been asked to join the team."

When pressed to explain how they "know" whether a
person will be successful, superior managers usually end
up by saying something like, "The qualities are intangible, but I know them when I see them." They have difficulty being explicit because their selection process is
intuitive and is based on interpersonal intelligence that
is difficult to describe. The key seems to be that they are
able to identify subordinates with whom they can probably work effectively—people with whom they are com-
patible and whose body chemistry agrees with their own.
They make mistakes, of course. But they give up on a
subordinate slowly because that means giving up on

themselves—on their judgment and ability in selecting, training, and motivating people. Less effective managers select subordinates more quickly and give up on them more easily, believing that the inadequacy is that of the subordinate, not of themselves.

Developing Young People

Observing that his company's research indicates that "initial corporate expectations for performance (with real responsibility) mold subsequent expectations and behavior," R.W. Walters, Jr., director of college employment at AT&T, contends that "initial bosses of new college hires must be the best in the organization."[9] Unfortunately, however, most companies practice exactly the opposite.

Rarely do new graduates work closely with experienced middle managers or upper-level executives. Normally they are bossed by first-line managers who tend to be the least experienced and least effective in the organization. While there are exceptions, first-line managers generally are either "old pros" who have been judged as lacking competence for higher levels of responsibility, or they are younger people who are making the transition from "doing" to "managing." Often these managers lack the knowledge and skill required to develop the productive capabilities of their subordinates. As a consequence, many college graduates begin their

Industry's greatest challenge is to rectify the underdevelopment, underutilization, and ineffective management and use of its most valuable resource—its young managerial and professional talent.

careers in business under the worst possible circumstances. Since they know their abilities are not being
developed or used, they quite naturally soon become
negative toward their jobs, employers, and business
careers.

Although most top executives have not yet diagnosed
the problem, industry's greatest challenge by far is to rectify the underdevelopment, underutilization, and ineffective management and use of its most valuable resource—
its young managerial and professional talent.

DISILLUSION AND TURNOVER

The problem posed to corporate management is under-
scored by the sharply rising rates of attrition among
young managerial and professional personnel. Turnover
among managers one to five years out of college is
almost twice as high now as it was a decade ago, and five
times as high as two decades ago. Three out of five companies surveyed by *Fortune* in the fall of 1968 reported
that turnover among young managers and professionals
is higher than five years ago.[10] While the high level of economic activity and the shortage of skilled personnel have
made job-hopping easier, the underlying causes of high
attrition, I am convinced, are underdevelopment and
underutilization of a workforce that has high career
aspirations.

The problem can be seen in its extreme form in the
excessive attrition rates of college and university graduates who begin their careers in sales positions. Whereas
the average company loses about 50% of its new college
and university graduates within three to five years, attrition rates as high as 40% in the *first* year are common

among college graduates who accept sales positions in the average company. This attrition stems primarily, in my opinion, from the failure of first-line managers to teach new college recruits what they need to know to be effective sales representatives.

As we have seen, young people who begin their careers working for less-than-competent sales managers are likely to have records of low productivity. When rebuffed by their customers and considered by their managers to have little potential for success, the young people naturally have great difficulty in maintaining their self-esteem. Soon they find little personal satisfaction in their jobs and, to avoid further loss of self-respect, leave their employers for jobs that look more promising. Moreover, as reports about the high turnover and disillusionment of those who embarked on sales careers filter back to college campuses, new graduates become increasingly reluctant to take jobs in sales.

Thus ineffective first-line sales management sets off a sequence of events that ends with college and university graduates avoiding careers in selling. To a lesser extent, the same pattern is duplicated in other functions of business, as evidenced by the growing trend of college graduates to pursue careers in "more meaningful" occupations, such as teaching and government service.

A serious "generation gap" between bosses and subordinates is another significant cause of breakdown. Many managers resent the abstract, academic language and narrow rationalization characteristically used by recent graduates. As one manager expressed it to me, "For God's sake, you need a lexicon even to talk with these kids." Nondegreed managers often are particularly resentful, perhaps because they feel threatened by the bright young people with book-learned knowledge that they do not understand.

For whatever reason, the generation gap in many companies is eroding managerial expectations of new college graduates. For instance, I know of a survey of management attitudes in one of the nation's largest companies that revealed that 54% of its first-line and second-line managers believed that new college recruits were "not as good as they were five years ago." Since what managers expect of subordinates influences the way they treat them, it is understandable that new graduates often develop negative attitudes toward their jobs and their employers. Clearly, low managerial expectations and hostile attitudes are not the basis for effective management of new people entering business.

INDUSTRY HAS NOT DEVELOPED effective first-line managers fast enough to meet its needs. As a consequence, many companies are underdeveloping their most valuable resource—talented young men and women. They are incurring heavy attrition costs and contributing to the negative attitudes young people often have about careers in business.

For top executives in industry who are concerned with organizational productivity and the careers of young employees, the challenge is clear: to speed the development of managers who will treat subordinates in ways that lead to high performance and career satisfaction. Managers not only shape the expectations and productivity of subordinates but also influence their attitudes toward their jobs and themselves. If managers are unskilled, they leave scars on the careers of young people, cut deeply into their self-esteem, and distort their image of themselves as human beings. But if they are skillful and have high expectations, subordinates' self-confidence will grow, their capabilities will develop, and their productivity will be high. More often than one realizes, the manager is Pygmalion.

Notes

1. The Rosenthal and Headstart studies are cited in Robert Rosenthal and Lenore Jacobson, *Pygmalion in the Classroom* (Holt, Rinehart, and Winston, 1968), p.11.

2. See John W. Atkinson, "Motivational Determinants of Risk-Taking Behavior," *Psychological Review,* vol. 64, no. 6, 1957, p. 365.

3. David E. Berlew and Douglas T. Hall, "The Socialization of Managers: Effects of Expectations on Performance," *Administrative Science Quarterly,* September 1966, p. 208.

4. Rosenthal and Jacobson, p. 3.

5. Berlew and Hall, p. 221.

6. David E. Berlew and Douglas T. Hall, "Some Determinants of Early Managerial Success," Alfred P. Sloan School of Management Organization Research Program #81-64 (MIT, 1964), p. 13.

7. Robert T. Davis, "Sales Management in the Field," HBR January–February 1958, p. 91.

8. Alfred A. Oberlander, "The Collective Conscience in Recruiting," address to Life Insurance Agency Management Association annual meeting, Chicago, Illinois, 1963, p. 5.

9. "How to Keep the Go-Getters," *Nation's Business,* June 1966, p. 74.

10. Robert C. Albrook, "Why It's Harder to Keep Good Executives," *Fortune,* November 1968, p. 137.

Originally published in January 2003
Reprint R0301G

About the Contributors

DAVID H. BURNHAM, at the time this article first appeared, was President and Chief Executive Officer at McBer Company, a behavioral science consulting firm. He is now a principal of the Burnham Rosen Group in Boston, where he continues to research what constitutes superior leadership and, through his firm, has been responsible for developing leaders in scores of organizations throughout the world.

BRONWYN FRYER is the senior West Coast editor for the *Harvard Business Review*. Previously, she was an award-winning independent journalist whose work appeared in *Newsweek, The New York Times, Fortune,* and many other publications.

At the time this article was originally published, **FREDERICK HERZBERG,** Distinguished Professor of Management at the University of Utah in Salt Lake City, was head of the department of psychology at Case Western Reserve University in Cleveland. His writings include the book *Work and the Nature of Man* (World, 1966).

STEVE KERR is the Chief Learning Officer at Goldman Sachs in New York. Prior to joining Goldman Sachs in 2001, he spent seven years as the chief learning officer and head of leadership development at GE. He was responsible for GE's leadership development center at Crotonville.

HARRY LEVINSON is Chairman Emeritus of the Levinson Institute and Clinical Professor of Psychology Emeritus in the Department of Psychiatry, Harvard Medical School.

J. STERLING LIVINGSTON was on the faculty of Harvard Business School from 1941 to 1971. He founded the Sterling Institute, a management consulting firm specializing in executive training and development, in 1967 and served as chairman of the Washington, DC–based institute until 1998. He is currently establishing the Sterling Center for Applied Managerial Leadership in Key Biscayne, Florida.

BROOK MANVILLE is the Chief Learning Officer of Saba Software, a provider of software and services for human capital development and management based in Redwood Shores, California. **JOSIAH OBER** is the David Magie Professor of Classics and the acting director of the University Center for Human Values at Princeton University in New Jersey. This essay is adapted from their book, *A Company of Citizens: What the World's First Democracy Teaches Leaders About Creating Great Organizations* (Harvard Business School Press, 2003).

At the time this article was originally published, **DAVID C. MCCLELLAND** was a professor of psychology at Harvard University.

NIGEL NICHOLSON is a professor of organizational behavior and the director of the Center for Organizational Research at London Business School. In recent years he has pioneered the application of evolutionary psychology to business in many writings, including "How Hardwired Is Human Behavior?" (*Harvard Business Review*, July–August 1998) and in his book *Managing the Human Animal* (Texere, 2000). His current research focuses on leadership in family firms, and the role of personality in executive development. He is a sought-after public speaker, a frequent contributor to newspapers and other media, and director of several executive programs, including High Performance People Skills and the innovative Proteus Program at London Business School. He consults to a wide variety of business organizations.

Index